D0583276

THE REFERENCE SHELF VOLUME 45 NUMBER 1

AFTERMATH OF COLONIALISM

EDITED BY
NANCY L. HOEPLI

Senior Editor, Foreign Policy Association

THE H. W. WILSON COMPANY
NEW YORK **1973**

THE REFERENCE SHELF

The books in this series contain reprints of articles, excerpts from books, and addresses on current issues and social trends in the United States and other countries. There are six separately bound numbers in each volume, all of which are generally published in the same calendar year. One number is a collection of recent speeches; each of the others is devoted to a single subject and gives background information and discussion from various points of view, concluding with a comprehensive bibliography. Books in the series may be purchased individually or on subscription.

Library of Congress Cataloging in Publication Data

Hoepli, Nancy L   comp.
   The aftermath of colonialism.

   (The Reference shelf, v. 45, no. 1)
   Bibliography: p.
   1. World politics--1945-   --Addresses, essays,
lectures. 2. States, New--Addresses, essays, lectures.
I. Title. II. Series.
D843.H625   327'.09'04   73-1618
ISBN 0-8242-0470-0

PREFACE

The age of decolonization is almost at an end. Except for a few vestigial remains, the great empires of Britain and France, Belgium, the Netherlands, and Spain have been overwhelmed by the independence movements that have swept across Asia and Africa since the outbreak of World War II.

In a quarter of a century an average of one new nation was born every five months—more than sixty-five all told. First to achieve independence were former British, French, and Dutch colonies along the southern periphery of Asia. As a result of postwar power realignments, sixteen nations, including India, Pakistan, and Indonesia, gained their independence between 1943 and 1951. The second great surge of independence, from 1956 through 1960, ended foreign rule in most of Africa, as twenty-four more countries joined the community of nations. The third wave of independence has brought freedom to another two dozen countries scattered through Africa, southern Asia and the Caribbean.

Today there are no colonies left in Asia, with the exception of a few military bases and trade centers (Macao, Timor, Hong Kong). In Africa, only a handful of Portuguese colonies remains. The new nations range in size from small islands—Western Samoa, Malta, Tobago—to the Philippines and Indonesia, from tiny Togo to India. They cover almost a fourth of the world's land area (except Antarctica) and contain more than one third of its population.

Sometimes the transition came by accommodation and sometimes by violent confrontation, but in almost every case the first years of independence were turbulent. With few exceptions constitutional government in the emergent nations proved fragile. A majority succumbed to rule by a single party or by the military. Of fourteen colonies which achieved independence by the mid-1950s, the governments

3

of eleven have been overthrown or threatened by illegal power grabs.

Most of the new nations are beset by a host of problems, among the most urgent of which is the need to forge a sense of national identity. Colonial boundaries tended to be arbitrary, encompassing peoples of different religions and different languages, with conflicting ethnic and cultural ties. The need is for the kind of political unity that will prevent these differences from deteriorating into costly and bloody civil wars. Still another major challenge is the establishment of stable government and workable political institutions which can function under the rule of law, rather than by the barrel of a gun. At the same time, the new nations must find ways to improve the standard of living of their desperately poor, rapidly growing populations.

The multitude of problems the new nations confront, their political instability and unfulfilled economic expectations, their violent rejection, in many cases, of ties with the former mother country—all these factors—would appear to make them tempting prospects for Soviet communism or subversion by people's wars. To date, Soviet and Chinese efforts to capitalize on the new states' weaknesses and to fill the vacuum left by the erosion of Western influence have met with only limited success. Emotional nationalism, reflected in the new nations' rejection of much of their colonial heritage, has found expression not in new alliances with the East but in neutralism.

Although the age of colonialism is near its end, the drama of its aftermath continues to unfold. Some of the highlights of that drama are told in the following pages.

The editor would like to thank the authors, publishers, and organizations represented in this compilation for their contributions.

NANCY L. HOEPLI

February 1973

CONTENTS

IV. ECONOMIC MODERNIZATION

V. Postscript to Colonialism

I. THE SEARCH FOR IDENTITY

EDITOR'S INTRODUCTION

One of the painful lessons of the postcolonial period for the leaders of the new Afro-Asian states is that independence does not always make a nation. Nationhood suggests a sense of national identity, unity, and purpose. Many of the new countries lack one or all of these attributes.

Black Africa, in part because it was influenced by the onslaught of European ways more than the Asian countries, has had a particularly difficult time resolving its problems of identity. On the one hand, it seeks to "Africanize" everything from place names to industry. On the other, it remains heavily dependent on the West. The one legacy of the white invasion which Africa has unequivocally embraced is change, according to the first article in this section, by Stanley Meisler, Africa correspondent of the Los Angeles *Times* for over a decade. And change is the one constant in Africa since independence.

The search for identity takes various forms. In black Africa, the search is symbolized by the current debate over whether to reject European languages in favor of tribal tongues. The debate is described by the New York *Times* correspondent William Borders. In North Africa, the conflict is between the pull of the Arab world and Islam and the pull of stronger ties with France, according to the London *Economist*.

The problem of national identity is not restricted to the African continent. In Asia, Malaysia, which achieved independence from Britain in 1957, is still grappling with the problem of blending three "nations" (Chinese, Malayan, and Indian) into one state. Nancy L. Snider explains the conflict in an *Asian Survey* article.

A strong, charismatic leader can play a decisive role in forging a sense of national identity. Kwame Nkrumah of Ghana was such a leader, according to St. Clair Drake's article in the *Nation*. Another is Hastings Banda, paternalistic leader of the small Central African country of Malawi. Ray Vicker of the *Wall Street Journal* describes this "offbeat nationalist," the grandfather of his country, in the final selection.

BLACK AFRICA: A DECADE OF CHANGE [1]

Ten years ago, I left New York on a dark, snow-lashed night and stepped down the next day into the morning glare of Dakar, in Senegal. It was an exciting, expectant time for the newly independent countries of Africa. Since that moment in Dakar, I have spent most of the last decade in Africa. Those ten years did not transform a gullible fool into a mean and narrow cynic, but I feel more critical, more doubtful, more skeptical, more pessimistic than I did in 1962. I still feel sympathetic and understanding. But I have learned that sympathy and understanding are not enough. Africa needs to be looked at with cold hardness as well.

There have been more disappointments than accomplishments in Africa in the ten years. Two events—the Nigerian civil war and the assassination of Tom Mboya—struck like body blows at the sympathies of an outsider. The war was probably the greatest scourge in black Africa since the slave trade, and it was largely self-made. Murder cut down the man who seemed most to represent all that was modern in new Africa, and it was probably done for the glory of tribal chauvinism.

On top of this, the decade has produced a host of other unpleasant events: the bloodshed in the Sudan, the barbaric chaos in the Congo and the rise to power of an Emperor Jones to give it stability, the mass slaughter of the graceful

[1] Article entitled "Black Africa," by Stanley Meisler, Africa correspondent of the Los Angeles *Times. Atlantic.* 230:10-15. Ag. '72. Copyright © 1972, by The Atlantic Monthly Company, Boston, Mass. Reprinted with permission.

Tutsis in Rwanda and the mass slaughter by the graceful Tutsis in neighboring Burundi, the procession of comic coups, the foolish posturing of weak little countries and weak little men, the interminable rhetoric, the faltering economies, the faltering governments, the faltering leaders.

While there have been achievements—the relative economic health of Kenya is one—independent black Africa is still the poorest, least organized place in the world, with weak central governments and unsophisticated economies in its plethora of little states. In fairness, Africa is at a stage of development where the differences between stability and chaos and between economic health and disaster are narrower than in the more sophisticated countries with stronger institutions. Nevertheless, Africa has slipped below the lines of difference too often.

There are historical arguments that are sometimes made to rationalize what seems like a sorry record. It is sometimes said, for example, that the record of Africa is no different from that of the so-called civilized world, that it is unfair for outsiders to hold Africa to a standard that European civilization has failed to meet. No savagery in Africa in the last decade matches that of the civilized Germans thirty years ago. No political murders in Africa match the senselessness of those in the United States. The only thing that makes Africa seem worse is the white man's deep, irrational repugnance for and dread of blackness.

A second argument begs for time. It describes Africa as passing through, though at an accelerated rate, the same phases as medieval Europe before the full creation of European nations and nationalism. African leaders have taken on the Herculean task of trying to weld nations out of hostile tribes forced into the same country by the artificial boundaries drawn by indifferent European imperialists. It took the Anglo-Saxons, Jutes, Danes, and Normans centuries to become the English, and the nationalism was forged from much bloodshed, instability, and cruelty. Why, or so the argument goes, expect the Africans to do the job immaculately?

Legacy

There is a good deal of force in both arguments, but I am uneasy with them. They seem to suppose that Africa is developing in a vacuum, condemned to repeat the ills and evils of white development. Perhaps there will be a repetition. But there certainly is no vacuum. There would be no new Africa today without the outside forces that have swept this continent into turmoil in a hundred years or so.

Yet, if you do not accept these historical arguments, what are you left with? A smug conclusion that Africans are doomed to incompetence, failure, disaster? A cynical feeling that all the attention, aid, and advice now lavished on Africa are worthless, too feeble to halt its incessant rush back to darkness? I do not think so.

I have come to the conclusion that Africa has to be understood by looking at it in a different way. Instead of counting coups and shaking his head, an outsider ought to stand apart and try to sense the intensity of a great historical movement there, for the only constant in Africa is change.

Change is a legacy of the invasion of the whites. For more than a century, the white man has come to Africa, as slave trader, merchant, explorer, missionary, conqueror, administrator, settler, and adviser. Confrontation with the whites has scarred the psychology of Africans, implanting a feeling of inferiority in them. The relationship between white and black in Africa, then and now, has always seemed fixed for me by an engraving in Henry M. Stanley's century-old book, *How I Found Livingstone in Central Africa*. It shows an African porter crossing a river with a box on his head. Stanley, in pith helmet, stands on the bank and points a revolver at the terrified black man. "Look out," Stanley says. "You drop that box—I'll shoot you."

Kinder white men than Stanley only substituted paternalism for cruelty. A glance at the writings of Dr. Albert Schweitzer provides an insight into a prevailing white attitude. "The Negro is a child," Schweitzer wrote in 1921, after his first years of work in Africa, "and with children nothing

can be done without the use of authority. . . . With regard
to the Negroes, then, I have coined the formula: 'I am your
brother, it is true, but your elder brother.' " It is pointless to
latch on to these words as more evidence to debunk
Schweitzer. He merely reflected a truth of his times. The
white man, in fact, did act, at best, as the elder brother of
the black man.

More important, the African, with incredible enthusiasm,
accepted the role of younger brother. Whatever the white
man did or had—schools, speech, clothes, religion, cars—the
black man mimicked or wanted. In Uganda, the "native
dress" of the Baganda women today is the floor-length Victorian frock introduced by missionary wives in the nineteenth century. Even the mass anticolonial movements that
brought on the rush to independence in the late 1950s and
early 1960s came from the adoption of Western democratic
ideas learned in the schools of Europe and America.

Of course, the degree of acceptance of white ways varied
from tribe to tribe and area to area. The Ibos of Nigeria
and the Kikuyus of Kenya, who had societies that awarded
status to a man for what he achieved in life and not for
what his ancestors did before him, were quick to see that
missionary education and the white man's commerce would
give them achievement and status and power. The degree
of mimicry also varied with the number of whites who settled
near the Africans. The Senegalese of Dakar—a French administrative center and settlement—became far more Western than the Voltans of Ouagadougou—a remote hardship
outpost in the French colonial empire. Muslim tribes, who
already had succumbed to a foreign culture, felt strong
enough to resist the white man and his Christianity. Nomads,
who wandered away from the white administrators and
settlers, did not feel the white impact as much as the farmers
who stood still.

But, despite these variations, a generalization can be
made. Africa, unlike Asia, put up little resistance to the onslaught of new ways during colonial days and has put up

even less since independence. There probably has been nothing like it since the millions of immigrants rushed into the United States in the late nineteenth century and gave up their culture and language for something new. There are, in fact, striking parallels. Just as immigrants from Jewish or Italian villages once formed village associations for security against the pressures of terrifying change in New York, African immigrants from the rural tribal lands now form tribal associations for security against the terrifying pressures of change in the African towns. An outsider's excitement about Africa these days probably comes from the wonder of seeing so much change so rapidly so near, and his despair comes from feeling all the failures and bitterness and conflict that have accompanied the change.

Back to Which Africa?

Nairobi, the city in which I now live, shows in an exaggerated way what change means. When I first came to Nairobi ten years ago, before Kenya, the white man's colony, became independent, it seemed like a lovely, cool English city, with Indian shopkeepers and clerks and barbers and cashiers living and working there under English sufferance. The only Africans a visitor really noticed in downtown Nairobi were sullen and cold men on street corners with nothing to do. The Africans, even though they supplied all the unskilled labor, seemed like tattered hangers-on. Nairobi was not their city.

Today, when I walk in downtown Nairobi in the late afternoon after the government offices close, the streets rush and bustle with young Africans in English suits and white shirts and thin conservative ties long out of style in America. Blacks drive their cars through town. Sometimes the cars are outrageously ostentatious for a poor African country. The chic African girls sport miniskirts and Afro wigs. The wigs attract them not because they are African but because they are Western.

All this depresses Africanists who like their Africa pure. The blacks of Nairobi, not long out of their tribal home- lands, are imitating the white people around them. They have adopted white dress and manners and values. Just like middle-class Englishmen, they prize a car, a television set, a house, good clothes, and short lines at the post office. They show off their English rather than their Swahili. Nairobi is decried again by Africanists as the new town of black white men.

At times, African politicians and intellectuals try to stop the relentless adoption of white ways. The attempt, in fact, can be so extreme that it turns almost comic. In a search for what he calls "authentic nationalism," President Joseph Désiré Mobutu of the Congo recently changed the name of his country to Zaïre and his own name to Mobutu Sese Seko Kuku Ngbendu Wa-za-Banga and ordered all Zaïreois to fol- low his example. More often, African leaders, such as Presi- dent Idi Amin of Uganda, ban what they look on as un- desirable imports from the white Western world—miniskirts, hot pants, and maxis with a V-shaped slit down the front.

The moves are popular, for Africans resent the superior white man whom they are trying to imitate. But they are also futile. They are a little like Mussolini's attempt to bring back the glory and grandeur of Rome by hanging fasces on his buildings. In fact, the African attempt may be even more futile, for Africa has no ancient Rome to bring back.

Some Africans understand this. The *Daily Nation* in Nairobi recently carried a letter from Omondi wa Radoli, an African reader annoyed by all the campaigns against miniskirts and hot pants:

Is the miniskirt African? No, neither are Mercedes cars, lifts, bell-bottoms, films and what have you. There are so many things un-African in our society that we are not justified in raising a hue about the mini only. Weren't African women wearing a flap of skin at the front and the back long ago? Aren't minis and hot pants much better, then?

. . . The African must wake up and discard his hypocrisy, and cease to bury his head in the sand and face facts as they stand —that is that African culture is gone. . . .

I suppose that this is depressing. While the developed world is growing disenchanted with modernity and searching for real and older values, Africans are dropping their traditional values in a frenzied scramble for all that seems modern to them. This is a force that no amount of hand-wringing by foreign romantics or culture-seeking by African intellectuals or name-swapping (as by the Congolese) can stop.

The main question now is, how deep and lasting are the changes? It is difficult to answer. Old British settlers in Kenya like to mutter that it will take centuries before the Africans learn to farm in modern ways or fly a jet plane or run a postal service as efficiently as the British do. But this seems like raw prejudice. The American experience has shown that it can take no more than a generation or two to transform a family from one culture to another, provided that there is an intense desire for change.

"Observe and Record"

Nevertheless, there is troubling evidence that change in Africa can be misdirected and pointless and sometimes superficial. It is easy, for example, to despair over African education, which is the major agent in modern Africa for implanting Western ways.

A Peace Corps volunteer once told me a story that symbolized for him all his woes in trying to teach African pupils at a secondary school in Cameroon. He introduced a chemistry experiment one day by writing across the blackboard: "Observe and record what happens." Every pupil dutifully took out his notebook and wrote down: "Observe and record what happens." African education is in the iron grip of rote.

It is not difficult to understand. African children, perhaps poorly nourished, weakened by worms, begin modern education by trekking from their huts to a strange and foreign school, their frightening gateway to the modern world. In a few years, their teachers, in a foreign language, usually English or French, have attacked them with a terrifying array of unfamiliar facts that have no relation to their world of rural villages. The teacher, for example, may print the word "boat" on the blackboard. But what is this word "boat"? They have never seen a boat or even a picture of one.

To cope with all this, the children scribble the facts into their notebooks and memorize them. There is very little else they can do. Once the facts are noted and memorized, the children have some power over them, though no understanding of them. This power gives the African child security. By the time he enters secondary school, he is a secure and successful rote learner, eager to write down and memorize everything that the teacher puts on the blackboard.

The process continues, even to the university. As a result, African education is producing a host of managers who sit in their government offices and meet every problem with their store of memories. If the problem is new, if memory fails to cope with it, the educated men shuffle it and then tuck it under the bottom of the mounting stack of papers on the desk.

African education does worse than create rote learners. It also produces an elite class alienated from the peasant life that traps most Africans. European education opens up a modern world to schoolboys, and they quickly turn their back on the old world. They are the elite of a backward society, and like most whites they meet in Africa, they intend to command servants, keep their hands free of toil, wear starched white shirts, and read European newspapers.

I once visited a Peace Corps volunteer at an agricultural secondary school in Tanzania and found that he was the only one who worked on the school farm. The students—presumably Tanzania's future agricultural bureaucrats—had no intention of dirtying their hands with the soil. The economy of Senegal has steadily deteriorated since independence because the country is run by a class of elite bureaucrats who every day spend a few hours in their offices in pleasant, cos-

mopolitan Dakar, mulling over the fashions and politics of
Paris. The uncomfortable, sandy, baking interior of Senegal
does not interest them.

All this leads to a great danger. Change may come so
swiftly that Africans will find themselves unable to cope with
it. Nigeria, for example, is black Africa's largest state and
has its most sophisticated economy. The civil war, however,
weakened its most adaptable and modernizing people, the
Ibos of Biafra. At the same time, the war and the postwar
boom in oil production have created new demands for services, and a more complex apparatus to supply them. Outsiders often feel that the Nigerians are now unable to manage the apparatus. Goods pile up in the port of Lagos and
the warehouses of the airport. Visitors find little or no water
in the main hotels. Flight reservations fail to find their way
to the check-in counters. At times, only bribes can unclog
the Nigerian machine. In short, the Nigerians have failed
to change enough as managers to cope with the problems
caused by the way in which they have changed as consumers.

At the moment, the only healthy control of the rate of
change in black Africa probably comes from the continued
presence of whites there. In some countries, such as the Ivory
Coast, there are more whites now than before independence.
It is a neocolonial and ironic situation, which is sure to of-
fend blacks and white liberal ideologues. But it is probably
necessary.

There is a good deal wrong with having crowds of white
advisers and managers around in Africa. Many still display
the attitudes of Stanley and Schweitzer. Many are poor teachers, preferring to manage a problem themselves rather than
help a black man learn to do it. They depress the self-confidence of blacks and often make them too dependent on
outsiders. Present a difficult problem to a black man in a
government office, and he will often send you to the white
adviser.

On balance, however, the whites probably help Africa—
even if perversely. By standing in the way of African ad-

vancement, they force younger Africans to get more experience than younger Africans feel they need for management.
By constantly expressing Western values and attitudes, they
hold up a standard that guides the change that is going on.

All this is resented by Africans, a natural reaction. It is
hard both to imitate and like the man who has the job you
want. The situation sometimes arouses so much suspicion
that a black man may refuse good advice just because it's
white advice.

It would be straining evidence to claim that the sorry
record of independent black Africa—coups, corruption, stagnation, mismanagement, slaughter—was the inevitable result
of change. Nothing can excuse the attempt of the Tutsi lords
in Burundi this year to wipe out the educated class of Hutus
there by killing more than fifty thousand of them. The evidence shows only that change so far has not been very orderly
or efficient or peaceful.

But ten years in Africa have taught me that the process
of change may be more important in the long run than the
disorder and waste that accompany it now.

THE LANGUAGE DEBATE [2]

All over black Africa people are talking about what language they should be talking.

The discussion centers on the question whether a proud,
independent nation should retain the language it learned
from the colonialists or go back to tribal languages.

"To parade around in a foreign language forever is merely
to parade our former slave status," the Nigerian columnist
Tunde Williams asserted in the Nigerian *Observer*, arguing
for the adoption of a native tongue to replace English.

In Dakar, Senegalese film makers are beginning to show
a preference for the Wolof language rather than French, and
airline stewardesses in Nairobi announce take-offs and land-

[2] From "For Africa, a Debate in Many Tongues," by William Borders,
staff correspondent. New York *Times*. p 1+. F. 28, '72. © 1972 by The New
York Times Company. Reprinted by permission.

ings in Swahili even though it is a safe assumption that the passengers can understand English.

"It's part of the need to be our own people, and I guess it's natural that we should suddenly become aware of it now, ten years or so after independence," said a student at the University of Abidjan, in the Ivory Coast, a citadel of French influence, where a new course in a local tongue, Dioula, has attracted a flood of applicants.

Perhaps a thousand distinct languages are spoken in Africa, and since the boundaries are usually ethnic boundaries as well, discussion of them usually touches on tribal and regional hostilities, which can charge any argument with great emotion.

Why the Conflicts

Thus it is that General Idi Amin, ruler of Uganda, wants to do away with English but rules out Swahili as a substitute because it is spoken in neighboring Tanzania and Kenya. Advocates of a common tongue in Lagos bicker about whether it should be Hausa, Yoruba or Ibo, Nigeria's major languages.

A hundred other tongues are spoken in Nigeria, and that fact, typical of Africa, is a reason why some people think few nations will be able to agree on the adoption of a single tribal language.

Said a Nigerian who expects to hear English spoken for a long time: "It was easy enough to agree to change the name of Broad Street to Yakubu Gowon Street as long as General Gowon is in power, but if they had tried to translate 'broad' into one of the local languages, the other tribes would have been on their necks." Thirty-five of the forty-three independent African countries use English or French as an official language; Arabic is spoken in most of the others.

In every case only the small urban elite uses the European language, conducting government and business in it. The overwhelming majority are fluent only in their tribal tongues, and their communication tends to be limited to the patch of desert or jungle or swamp where their ancestors lived.

To the distress of some nationalists, the first layer of education usually involves the European language rather than the tribal language of the man who lives across the way.

A young eastern Nigerian employed as a driver by an American visitor to Lagos took him to Cotonou, the sleepy capital of the former French colony of Dahomey, eighty miles away. Once there the Nigerian was shocked to discover that without help he could not even bargain with his fellow Africans over the price of a pineapple. They spoke Yoruba and a bit of French; he spoke Ibo and rather good English. The visitor, a white who could speak the two colonial languages, was needed to bridge the gap.

Advocates of African languages maintain that barriers like that will be broken by concentration on local tongues, less on English and French.

Kenya Encourages Swahili

Kenya, for example, is encouraging the use of Swahili as a substitute not only for English, which is widely regarded as neocolonialist, but also for Kikuyu and Luo, which are used in certain sections of the country.

Because no country in Africa has only one language, people in business and government spend a lot of time working in a language other than their own. Still, no imposed common tongue has met with much success, although some uniformity has been nurtured by the ubiquitous transistor radio and by the natural movement of people—like the traders who carried the Lingala dialect long distances up and down the jungled banks of the Congo River. . . .

What Schools Teach

In the schools, which still reach only a small proportion of African children, the European languages predominate, but there too a strong faction among the teachers favors the use of the vernacular, especially in the primary grades.

"The moment you're trying to explain something at all complicated—math, for example—you have to slip into the tribal language anyway or you know the child won't follow you," said a teacher in Liberia, where English is the teaching language.

Few African leaders, even the most militant, have taken the side of those who want to do away with the colonial languages. . . .

Since few of the tribal languages are spoken by more than two million or three million people, some think that there is little alternative to the European languages.

As a West African politician put it: "English is an imperfect medium here, but it's still a damn sight better than any of the other choices open to us."

THE MAGHREB: ARAB OR EUROPEAN? [3]

A girl walks down a street in Algiers. She wears, like millions of others throughout the world, a maxicoat, a minidress and a headscarf tied under her chin. But she is different. The lower part of her face is hidden by a fine, beige veil. She is followed by stares and smiles, for the women of North Africa either retain their traditional dress or blossom out in the latest European styles. But this girl's idiosyncrasy illustrates two features which distinguish the countries of the Maghreb—Morocco, Algeria and Tunisia—from the remainder of North Africa and the rest of the Arab world.

The Arab word *maghreb* means west and the term has long been used to denote the western wing of the Arab-speaking world. But it is applicable in another sense. On the northern shores of the western Mediterranean the people and the cultures of the east and west have met and mingled. The Europeans may feel that the east begins at Tangier, just nine miles from the tip of Spain. But Tangier is as near the United States as London is and it might be argued that

[3] From article, "Maghreb: A Survey," by Michael Wall, foreign correspondent, in collaboration with Sue Dearden. *Economist* (London). 242:survey p 3. Mr. 11, '72. Reprinted by permission.

Europe's southernmost boundary is not its Mediterranean shore but the Middle Atlas mountains.

The fruits of the Maghreb's geographical closeness to Europe and its historical ties with France, Spain and Italy are very much in evidence in the urban societies of the Maghreb today. In Tunis, Algiers and Casablanca it is easy to imagine that one is in a French provincial city complete with its traffic jams, café life and language. Yet the influences of the Arab world and Islam are there too, and the pull of east and west, especially on the younger generations, creates unavoidable tensions. To which world do they belong?

After years of colonial occupation the Maghreb is now on its own. In each country there are forces pulling its people both ways at once. There are those who believe that to establish their own national identity the links with the east must be strengthened—that now the colonialists are gone the future must lie with the Arab world and its religion, language and culture. There are others who feel that the ties with Paris are stronger than those with Cairo or Damascus and they regard efforts to make their society Arab as a step back into a dead past. And in each of the countries which today make up the Maghreb there are voices, admittedly not as yet very strong, who say that Morocco, Algeria and Tunisia have a unique opportunity to forge ahead through closer cooperation and eventual unity among themselves. A united Maghreb could, they argue, blend the best from east and west and need not turn away from either.

MALAYSIA: ONE STATE, THREE "NATIONS" [4]

The conflict between the concepts of nation and state in the postwar worlds of Asia and Africa has been of deep and lasting concern to social scientists. Those of us interested in Southeast Asia have witnessed in many instances the tragic practical results which stem from incongruity between these

[4] From "Race, Leitmotiv of the Malayan Election Drama," by Nancy L. Snider, assistant professor of political science, University of Wisconsin/Stevens Point. *Asian Survey*. 10:1070-4. D. '70. © 1970 by The Regents of the University of California. Reprinted by permission of The Regents.

two concepts. But perhaps in no country save Nigeria has a greater attempt been made to ignore this incongruity, with more disastrous results, than in ... Malaysia.

Indeed the most serious aspects of the problem can be limited even further to West Malaysia, comprising the Malayan peninsula only. . . . The crux of the state-nation disparity in the Malaysian case is most clearly evidenced at this point in time in the divergent world-views held by the almost equally powerful Chinese and Malay "nations" of mainland Malaya.

In Malaya, national identity has evolved around primordial concepts of race, language, and/or religion. These exert a strong centripetal force toward association with others of like primordialisms within Malaya, and a strong centrifugal force toward identification with the homeland country . . . (i.e. Indonesia, China, and India). Under these circumstances, the attempt to establish and intensify something called Malayan or Malaysian national identity . . . becomes an attempt to make bricks without straw. In Malaya's brief fifteen years of independence, strains and tensions arising from the lack of a sense of national identity have been to some extent papered over by the fiction of a cooperative tripartite Alliance Party and government. This party operated the civil state structure for the purported benefit of all races. It was successful up to a point in brainwashing the party faithful, as well as quite a few others, Malaysians and foreigners alike, into believing that primordial tensions were being slowly sublimated and subsumed within the framework of a Malaysian national identity. Many of us *wanted* to believe this; therefore, it became an act of will to believe and a further act of will to try and ignore the many danger signals flashing along the way. But the signals were there—and as might be expected, they flashed the brightest during Malaya-Malaysia's four postwar elections.

If one defines the negative aspect of nationalism as "sentiment and activity opposed to alien control" . . . , it is clear that this negative aspect helped bind the strawless Malayan bricks together during two of the four election periods. In the 1955 elections, the anti-British *merdeka* (freedom) theme was almost the sole issue. In the 1964 elections, the Alliance attempted to make Indonesian *konfrontasi* the only issue, and to a great extent succeeded in so doing, much to the surprise of some observers. Thus the large rips in the Alliance fabric of primordial group cooperation, which had begun to show during the 1959 campaign, were successfully hidden in the 1964 elections behind a facade of anti-Sukarno unity.

By 1969, however, this element of negative nationalism was missing, and the rifts between the three Alliance sub-parties were being ever widened by extremist elements in all three groups. These elements were encouraged and stimulated during the campaign by the intensified racial appeals made by almost every opposition party without exception. . . .

There are some students of primordial or communal conflict in Malaysia (as well as some observers of black-white conflict in America) who have taken an unequivocal stand to the effect that these conflicts stem solely from socioeconomic stratification and economic class differences, rather than from racial or cultural differences and distinctions. I should state at the outset that I disagree with this viewpoint. . . . [It] seems probable that in the Malaysian case at least, cultural and sociological differences among the three main primordial groups are at least as important factors in communal conflict as economic and class factors. These differences may or may not bear any direct relation to economic position and social class. This is an important point to be considered, not only for Malaysia, but for other developing countries as well. I would suggest that it is an as yet unproved assumption that economic betterment *per se* for a segment of a multiracial polity—a segment distinguishable in terms of being a specific economically backward primordial group such as the Malays in Malaya—will automatically help ease communal frictions between this group and other groups in the polity. I would further suggest that where this assumption seems to be validated it may well be as much a

function of economic development bringing with it the acceptance of new (and *perhaps* Westernized) social and cultural patterns of thought and behavior by the backward
group . . . as it is a function of economic equality or increased economic opportunity *per se*.

The Malay-dominated Alliance Party, during its twenty-
year period of hegemony in Malayan-Malaysian politics,
seems to have accepted completely the assumption that racial
conflict could be avoided by programs to help the economically backward rural Malays improve their economic status.
It was one of the tacit agreements of the negotiations sur-
rounding the birth of the Malayan Federation 1957 that
Chinese domination of Malayan business would not be inter-
fered with, provided the Chinese cooperated in efforts to
improve the lot of the poor Malays. When racial outbursts
and incidents occurred later on therefore, the government
tended to put the blame on Communist agitation and/or a
lack of Chinese cooperation in helping the poor Malays economically. The Alliance Party majority coalition did little
or nothing over the years to encourage or even permit objective study and analysis of the varying sociological and
historical factors involved. . . . The attitude of the Alliance
toward the Malayan-Malaysian communal problem during
this period seemed to be similar to the attitude of at least
some segments of American official and popular opinion
toward the People's Republic of China during the first decade or so after the Communist takeover of the mainland—
"If we don't think about it, don't recognize it, and just ignore
it, it will (somehow) eventually go away."

However, there are some divisive Malaysian communal
issues that simply cannot be ignored or postponed. First in
rank order of such issues is the problem of language usage
and its derivative problem of medium of instruction in the
schools. This reflects in a very fundamental way the deep-
seated racial-cultural chauvinism of Malaya's communal
groups. In casting about in 1957 for some element . . . that
could be used to build a sense of national identity among

culturally diverse inhabitants of the Malayan peninsular "state," language was seized upon as perhaps the only plausible unifier. If agreement could have been obtained on English (or indeed on some other "neutral" language) as the National Language of Malaya, this unifier might have worked. But the agreement in 1957 was that Malay was to be the National Language of Malaya with the implication . . . that Malay would eventually become the sole official language and sole medium of instruction in the schools. The battle over a policy of permissive multilingualism versus Malay as the sole language has raged unabated since 1957. It was the wedge which splintered the MCA [Malaysian Chinese Association] in the 1959 pre-election period, and the bludgeon with which opposition parties battered the Alliance (and to some extent each other as well) during the 1969 election campaign and the months immediately preceding. In the tension-filled atmosphere of heated political campaigning, the struggle for multilingualism with its practical concomitant appeal for support for a Chinese-language "Merdeka University," began to symbolize the entire range of Malay-Chinese-Indian divergencies. . . . Intense polarization and racial rioting *cum* civil chaos were the unfortunate results.

NKRUMAH: THE REAL TRAGEDY [5]

World attention first became fixed upon [Kwame] Nkrumah [former President of the Republic of Ghana, who died in exile in April 1972] in the early 1950s when the Gold Coast was granted internal self-government by Great Britain. The spotlight was focused sharply in March 1957 when the independent nation of Ghana was born, with Nkrumah as prime minister. President Eisenhower sent Vice President Nixon as his special envoy for the occasion, with an invitation to Nkrumah to visit the United States. In 1958, Ghana

[5] From article by St. Clair Drake, former head of the department of sociology, University of Ghana, currently professor of anthropology and sociology, Stanford University. *Nation*. 214:722-4. Je. 5, '72. Reprinted by permission.

was host to the First Conference of Independent African States (there were only eight!) and the First All-African Peoples Conference. . . .

Throughout 1954 and 1955, Nkrumah had been faced with the problem that was later to plague the Congo and Nigeria—the centripetal pull of tribalism and regionalism. With a popular vote base of 56 percent and with 72 of 104 seats in the legislative assembly, his CPP [Convention People's Party] passed a deportation act in 1957 aimed at Muslim religious leaders from neighboring states who were backing a Muslim Association Party; an antidiscrimination act that made it illegal to organize political parties based on religion, race, tribe or region; and a preventive detention bill that allowed individuals to be held for periods of up to five years without trial. At this point the Western press began to accuse the Ghanaian Prime Minister of having dictatorial inclinations and of suppressing civil liberties. He answered back in a broadcast six months after the independence celebrations:

> The first duty of a government is to govern. Hence the preservation of our internal security is paramount. I wonder if those abroad who have criticized us fully appreciate the problem in Ghana where we have to deal with a complex relationship of feudal tribes and other factors and where we have to fight against inspired rumors and vicious misrepresentations. It is obvious that we are dealing with conditions quite unlike those in many other countries. . . . Thus we must adopt methods appropriate to the problems we have to solve and still preserve the basic rights of the individual. . . . When the international press and radio comment on our affairs I hope they will keep facts such as these in mind.

American journalists gave Nkrumah a good press up to this point in 1957, intrigued as they were with a charismatic, *American-trained* African nationalist leader, but the preventive detention bill outraged Western values. However, that piece of legislation, like the others, was a direct response to information being supplied by Scotland Yard that certain members of the United Party were involved in an elaborate and mysterious plot; but no overt acts made it possible to arrest and charge them. I was at the University of Ghana from October 1958 to February 1961 and remember being cornered once for an hour by Ghana's British attorney general who was intent on explaining to me how he had lost cases against known plotters of political murder because his witnesses had been so terrified by "witch doctors" that they changed their stories. He insisted that he would not trust the security of the country to the possibility of getting a conviction under Anglo-Saxon legal procedures. Nkrumah was too proud to make that kind of defense of the bill.

Highly centralized and personalized leadership was not unique to Ghana. It is a general African phenomenon, reflecting high levels of illiteracy and the fragility of loyalties to the nation-state in societies where tribal and kinship ties are still the most cohesive social bonds and the authority of traditional chiefs is ubiquitous at local and regional levels. Nkrumah's Ghana, like most African states, was authoritarian; yet none of them is totalitarian in the European sense that one dominant political party becomes all-embracing, making voluntary associations illegal, and puts an efficient secret police system to work. Fears were expressed that Nkrumah's party was moving in that direction when it declared national trade union organizations and some women's and youth groups to be "integral wings" of the CPP, but there were always numerous voluntary associations. . . .

Nkrumah was accused of becoming increasingly repressive, and while the stories are exaggerated, it is true that in the three years preceding the coup, security measures were strengthened where the President's person was concerned. Again, there was nothing unique about this. Under constant pressures from their people to make a quick payoff on political promises, watching unemployed youth become more and more concentrated in the cities, unable to secure the large amounts of capital needed to move swiftly toward an industrial "takeoff," fearful of trade unionists and left-wing leaders who exploit tribal and regional parochialisms as well

as legitimate grievances, facing continuous international in-
trigue and occasional coups and army mutinies, the civilian
leaders of *all* African states, irrespective of ideology, become
more concerned with maintaining political stability, developing national integration, and fostering economic development than in guarding the civil liberties that concern only
a fraction of their people. Even formerly ardent liberals such
as the scholarly Julius Nyerere of Tanzania and the sensitive
and gentle Kenneth Kaunda of Zambia, have proven no different in this regard than Haile Selassie, Ethiopia's modernizing monarch, the conservative Tubman [of Liberia] or radicals such as Kwame Nkrumah and Sekou Touré [of Guinea].
When being compared leaders should perhaps be evaluated
in terms of the extent to which distributive justice is their
primary concern, rather than in terms of how "democratic"
in a Western sense they are. Psychoanalytical characteriza-
tions are particularly unrewarding. . . .

That Nkrumah thought of himself as a very special person with a mission is obvious; so is the fact that a lot of
other people thought so too. The interaction between him
and the people of Ghana was similar to that between de
Gaulle and the people of France. In neither case did the
charisma last forever, but even when it faded an affinity remained between leader and the led. That is why flags were
lowered to half-mast in Ghana when the Osagyefo [warrior
chief who defeated the enemy and saved the nation] died.
Nkrumah also had that stubborn streak of de Gaulle, Crom-
well, John Brown and Nat Turner. He knew his mission
and was sure he was right—only a Socialist United States of
Africa could solve the continent's problem. He never re-
treated from that position, but also during twenty-five years
of public life he never discovered how to integrate the rule
of statesmanlike administrator with that of leader of the
African Socialist revolution. He tried to conceptualize the
problem in dialectical terms and coined the expression "social contention" to apply to the inevitable conflict within a
party, movement—or nation—that can, nevertheless, be a

progressive force. In fact, Nkrumah was forced to change pace and obvious direction and often to conceal from the right hand what the left hand was doing. Thus his actions generated a sense of uneasiness among conservatives, of skepticism on the part of radicals, and perhaps of distrust generally. There was respect, even affection, for Nkrumah, but also deep-rooted distrust. That was the real tragedy of trying to play this dual role.

HASTINGS BANDA, OFFBEAT NATIONALIST [6]

[Malawi's] Life President Ngwazi Dr. Hastings Kamuzu Banda is the erudite father of this country. He seems likely to be its dictatorial grandfather, too, much to the annoyance of radical black nationalists further north who view him as an Uncle Tom.

That title *ngwazi* means "chief." Dr. Banda is unquestionably the boss in this little Central African country of 4.5 million. The last election confirmed him in the presidency for as long as he lives. And he uses his office to further his claim that a black-white confrontation is unnecessary in Africa, that a patient, black-white dialogue will gain much more in the long run for black Africans in Southern Africa.

That's counter to the views of the radicals in the Organization of African Unity. They've already decided that there can be no compromises with South Africa, Rhodesia and Portugal.

So Dr. Banda might seem to be African nationalism's odd-man-out. In an interview in the presidential lodge here, he makes it clear that he isn't going to be faced down by what he considers to be his inferiors in African nationalism. The lodge is a palatial red brick and glass structure set in a park-like glade. It is geared to the tastes of a Life President who has earned some of the perks of success through the years of struggle spent earlier in the cause of African nationalism.

[6] From article by Ray Vicker, chief European correspondent. *Wall Street Journal.* p 8. Ag. 29, '72. Reprinted with permission of *The Wall Street Journal.*

Dr. Banda is a five-foot-high bantam rooster of a man, who seems to grow in stature when he takes the floor. At sixty-six, his gray hair is so close-cropped that he sometimes looks bald. He is a Church of Scotland elder with puritan ethics and, like most puritans, he is convinced that God is on his side. Like many men, too, who have had to struggle for an education, he has a chip-on-shoulder aggressiveness. He isn't ready yet to apologize to any so-called African nationalist of today.

A Successful Triumvirate

He remembers that he formed a triumvirate with Ghana's Kwame Nkrumah and with Kenya's Jomo Kenyatta to launch African nationalism on its successful road when World War II ended. In his view, the African nationalism of the continent's left-leaning militants went astray when radical Arab influence was allowed to permeate black African organizations. He contends that it is naive for anybody in the Western world to accept such nationalism as the voice of the masses in Africa.

"Arabs are not Africans," he says bluntly. "During my father's time, the Arabs who came to Africa looked for slaves."

He irks African militants in many ways. Malawi has diplomatic relations with South Africa and Portugal. It accepts South African foreign aid. Moreover, Dr. Banda believes that Africa's leaders should look to the needs of their own peoples, first, before delving into the affairs of others.

That view especially rankles some radicals elsewhere, because Dr. Banda is showing them how to handle the job. Much as critics hate to admit it, Malawi's gross national product is rising at 10 percent a year. Since independence in 1964, its exports have more than doubled. One who has visited this country at least a dozen times in the last decade and a half can see easily that a once stagnant African laggard is moving ahead.

Much credit for that must go to Dr. Banda, for he is so much the boss of this little nation that he even dictates the length of the female skirt. The first notice to catch attention when a visitor lands at Chileka Airport near here is one about female dress. It says:

In Malawi, it is traditional for women not to appear in public in dresses that expose any part of the leg above the knee.

Accordingly, there is a restriction in Malawi on the wearing in public of dresses and skirts that do not fully cover the knee-cap when the wearer is standing upright. Also restricted for women are shorts and trousers worn in public.

Restrictions have been modified only for tourists who might be spending time at a Malawi resort. Dr. Banda, a man who doesn't drink or smoke, has no intention of allowing sin in the form of the miniskirt to tempt his people.

That puritan streak comes from his background. He learned his three Rs well in a mission school, working with a slate board and chalk. At thirteen he ran away from home to work in the mines of South Africa. There he saved enough for passage to the United States, and a hoped-for education. He arrived in New York with $10 in his pocket, and not even the equivalent of a high school education. Yet, he managed to work his way to a B.A. in philosophy at the University of Chicago and to medical degrees at Meharry Medical College, Nashville, Tennessee, and at Edinburgh University in Scotland. Among jobs when at school was that of part-time minister. Even today he could fill a pulpit in most churches, quoting his Bible from memory.

He practiced medicine in a white section of London for years. It was there that he rubbed shoulders with exiles Kenyatta and Nkrumah, and helped formulate African nationalistic policies with them. When a weary Britain started disengaging in Africa, Dr. Banda was ready to lead Nyasaland to independence as Malawi. (*Malawi* means "dawn," reflecting the mood of the people when independence arrived in 1964.)

An interview with Dr. Banda is always entertaining, always a mind bender. He is apt to fire questions back at the interviewer and he has a grasp of names, dates and facts which covers a broad range of subjects. So the interviewer sometimes feels like the Ph.D. candidate undergoing an oral examination with his professor.

He speaks so bluntly that one expects a warning that certain passages must be "off the record." Not so, with President Banda. Equivocation is not part of his nature. . . .

While Dr. Banda's views concerning violence seem solidly based on his church upbringing, there are strong economic reasons for cooperation with South Africa and Portugal. Malawi is a landlocked nation. Its only routes to the Indian Ocean are over the Portuguese Mozambique rail system to the ports of Nacala and of Beira.

Moreover, at any one time, 250,000 Malawians are outside the country, the bulk of them working in South Africa. The pay they send home forms a vital part of Malawi's foreign exchange. In Malawi, one hears many citizens speaking glowingly of the high pay for the blacks in South Africa, which is true when comparisons are made with wages in independent black Africa. Thus there is a residue of good feeling toward South Africa among Malawians which is hard for some outsiders to understand. Dr. Banda has been able to get away with his black-white dialogue policy because most Malawians favor it. They do not want those routes to jobs in the south eliminated through political differences.

A Victorian Patriarch

If he is a realist abroad, he is a realist in the Victorian style at home. With his own people, he is father sitting at the head of the table, ready to instruct the whole family as to how they should behave. Longhairs don't get any further here than does the miniskirt. Not long ago, Dr. Banda attacked expatriate teachers for their sloppy dress and unkempt hair. Said he: "They look like bandits and robbers, rather than teachers."

He skirmishes with progressive educators in the school system. Under British rule, Malawi had one of the highest literacy rates in Africa, and it was the intelligence of Malawians which made them so welcome in South Africa's mines. Then, as progressive methods of schooling were adopted, the nation's schools started turning out some high school graduates who couldn't read and spell. So Dr. Banda has turned the schools back to the McGuffey-reader type of education, with strong emphasis in early years on the ABCs.

He uses his own story to show that with a proper educational base a student may go through university. Says he: "There was nothing different about me. I was an ordinary boy from the bush. It was the teaching that made the difference. I was taught properly, step by step, and this has stayed with me all my life."

Not long ago at a graduation ceremony at the University of Malawi, he emphasized that standards in the university should be raised. It is better, said he, to produce a few well-educated graduates than to mass produce a lot of ill-trained grads who won't fit into society. This doesn't jibe with egalitarian concepts of education, either.

But then, Dr. Banda is not the type of man who follows the herd psychology whether it has to do with South Africa, or formal education. This makes him a target from many directions. It hardly seems to bother him at all. Says he: "I see situations as they are, not as we would wish them to be." And as to the complaints of some of his opponents, he says: "I know how to shout when the need arises, but I also know when to keep my mouth shut."

II. NATIONS DIVIDED: THE STRUGGLE FOR UNITY

EDITOR'S INTRODUCTION

Political unity has been a will o' the wisp in many of the newly independent Afro-Asian nations. In South and Southeast Asia, the region with the longest history of political independence, there is not a single government that has not had to contend with dissident groups. These disaffected minorities, united by bonds of language, religion, regional or ethnic loyalty, have undermined the authority of their governments by riots, insurrections, and small wars. The groups include the hill people of Burma, the Chinese and southern Malays in Thailand, the Vietnamese in Cambodia, the Pathans in Pakistan, language minorities in Ceylon and India.

Africa has also had its share of bloodshed stemming from tribal, religious, and regional conflicts. Although it appears well on the road to recovery, according to the optimistic account written by Albert J. Meyers in a 1970 issue of *U.S. News & World Report*, black Africa has been the scene of three devastating civil wars. Stanley Meisler reports on the Congo-Kinshasa [now Zaïre]; Ruth First, a South African living in exile in London, writes about Nigeria's civil war; and the Sudanese political scientist Muddathir 'Abd al-Rahim, analyzes the north-south split in his country. Sudan's sixteen-year-long civil war ended only in 1972.

The most recent victim of civil strife is Pakistan. The breakup of Pakistan, divided at independence into an east wing and a west wing separated by one thousand miles of Indian territory, and the birth of Bangladesh are the subject of Norman Palmer's essay, which follows.

Internal conflicts do not need to escalate into civil war to leave permanent scars on the body politic. Two recent examples, discussed in the final articles in this section, are the explosion of tribal tensions in Kenya following the murder of Tom Mboya, and the tragic slaughter of the Hutus by the Tutsis in Burundi, which temporarily shattered that country's hopes for building a multitribal state.

UP FROM CHAOS: BLACK AFRICA AFTER TEN YEARS OF FREEDOM [1]

Reprinted from *U.S. News & World Report.*

Travel around black Africa in 1970 and you find dramatic evidence almost everywhere of a change for the better.

Look back ten years to 1960, when seventeen African states gained independence in a single year.

Then, Africa seemed a dark, mysterious, even frightening part of the world. To many outsiders, it was no more than a vast jungle, dominated by hordes of black men unable to govern themselves.

Today, not all the old ways of doing things have died out completely. The world of witch doctors, poisoned arrows and jungle drums still exists.

But a new Africa is emerging at the same time to replace the old.

It is true that Nigeria still is paying heavily for its cruel civil war. The wounds of the Congo's bloodletting are not completely healed. And racial tension between black and white Africa remains high.

However, it is also true that for many African nations the era of violence is ending and is being succeeded by a period of economic development.

Toward Stability

Instead of political turmoil, civil wars and foreign intervention—real or threatened—at every turn, a correspondent

[1] From article by Albert J. Meyers, staff correspondent. *U.S. News & World Report.* 69:52-4. Jl. 6, '70.

who has watched this continent's painful emergence from colonialism now finds black leaders evolving African solutions for African problems. Some instances:

The average African in the thirty-six independent black African states is better off in 1970 than he was under colonial governments, if only because his own authorities pay closer attention to his desires than did the earlier, more remote administrations.

Political stability most often has been maintained by strong, military-backed presidents ruling one-party states with the support of the leading tribal group.

Far from becoming another arena for East-West competition, as seemed likely during the Congo crisis in the violent summer of 1960, black Africa gradually is slipping out of the mainstream of big-power confrontations.

The era of massive invasion of official foreign aid is coming to an end as the industrial powers' interest shifts elsewhere. Africans today are being left more to find their own solutions to problems.

For most African states, the 1960s were years of trial and error in development plans as priorities were sorted out and goals set.

More and more, the black countries have been moving down the Socialist path by taking over businesses formerly owned by foreigners—many of them Asians, chiefly Indians.

Ending now are the days when foreign companies could move into an African nation and take over control of important local industries. . . .

The Marks of War

Against this record of better economic prospects must be put the cost of ten years of civil and tribal warfare, and the collapse of Western-style democracies most African nations inherited with independence. . . .

At least 2.5 million people are estimated to have died in the continent's two major wars—in Nigeria and the Congo.

Strains are increasing between black-controlled North and Central Africa, and white-ruled areas to the south. In some regions, guerrilla fighting is likely to continue for years to come. . . .

Classic, parliamentary-type democracy has taken a hammering as the need for strong centralized government and political stability has seemed most important to national leaders.

Hardest of all, for many of these new states, has been the creation of a national feeling stronger than tribal ties.

Often little more than the historical accident of colonial administrations was responsible for existence of the separate states. This was true especially among former French colonies in West Africa.

Even so, few of these nations show valid signs of attaching themselves to richer neighbors. And the chance that some, at least, will find mineral riches within their frontiers seems sure to forestall any moves to form wider political associations.

The Congo Recovery

One country that appears to have survived a major attempt to split it apart is the Congo-Kinshasa. After years of disappointments and violence, things are much brighter for this vast area, as big as all of the United States east of the Mississippi but with a population of just 16 million people.

For almost the first time in ten years, an American can travel safely through most of the country. New cars, television sets and refrigerators are to be seen for sale in the stores of the capital, Kinshasa.

Copper output is hitting record levels and is set to expand 30 percent in the next few years. Exports of cotton are resuming this year after a ten-year break.

Even the devastated agricultural areas of the northern Congo are well on the way to recovery after being ruined by years of war. Prices, too, have reached a kind of stability, after rising as much as 90 percent.

Nigeria: Oil Helps

The scars of war are slowly on the mend in another of Africa's major nations, Nigeria.

For that country, the basis of recovery is oil production. Output is about one million barrels of crude oil a day and is expected to double in a year, pulling in hundreds of millions of dollars in hard currencies needed for development.

More problematical is Nigeria's political future. To many observers, the civil war was a sign of growing maturity, fought, as the Nigerians put it, "to keep Nigeria one," rather than allow it to fragment into tribal states.

Today, the problem is to make the slogan a reality and reintegrate the dissident Ibo tribe into national life. One by-product of the war was the creation of black Africa's largest army, now 150,000 strong. This army seems sure to go on playing a considerable political role.

CONGO: PAST AND PRESENT [2]

There are two ways of looking at the Congo. The first is to compare it with the past, and marvel. Once in turmoil, fractured, tearing apart, projecting images of brutality and savagery, the Congo these days is a reasonably calm, quiet, secure, and united country of twenty million people. A visitor can go almost anywhere without fear. The authority of President Joseph Désiré Mobutu reaches almost everywhere. Considering the Congo's history, these are remarkable achievements.

The second way of looking at the Congo is to put aside the past, take the Congo for what it is today, and despair. The Congo is exhibiting some of the worst traits of independent black Africa—corruption, waste, elitism, luxury, grandiosity, and neglect. The government can build what the Congolese call the world's second-largest swimming pool,

[2] From article entitled "The Congo," by Stanley Meisler, Africa correspondent of the Los Angeles *Times*. *Atlantic*. 227:26+. Mr. '71. Copyright © 1971, by The Atlantic Monthly Company, Boston, Mass. Reprinted with permission.

but it refused, for more than a year, to pay the bills to transport to the Eastern Congo US relief food for children afflicted
with kwashiorkor, the disease of advanced malnutrition. The
public treasury spends millions of dollars for monuments
and parades but no money to build a road from the farms
of Kivu Province to their port on the Congo River. At a
time when other African leaders, like President Julius
Nyerere of Tanzania, are trying to infuse their people with
self-reliance, austerity, and honesty, Mobutu is rushing the
Congo the other way.

Those who sympathize with Mobutu, including American officials, plead that an outsider must not let his second
way of looking at the Congo obscure the first. They insist
that waste is a small price to pay for security and that the
Congo, with its history of disunity and humiliation, and its
lack of confidence, may need circuses and monuments more
than other countries. This argument is hard to dismiss or
even discount, but it is based on some questionable assumptions. . . .

Today, Mobutu, wearing his leopard-skin cap and bran-
dishing a baroque cane, exudes confidence and authority.
Once an almost inaudible, frightened speaker, he now addresses adulating crowds of thousands for hours, his voice
hysterical, strident, yearning, cajoling, firm. There is a sure-
ness in his measured walk and a dignity in his bearing. His
authority was demonstrated . . . [in 1970] in the Congo's
sham presidential election. The final tally showed 10,131,669
votes for Mobutu and 157 against him. . . .

The whole style of Mobutu, the national hero and leader,
raises a number of questions and doubts. The first is whether
the creation of a national hero really is the sensible way to
unite a nation. Supporters of Kwame Nkrumah of Ghana
once rationalized his dictatorship this way. Yet his grandeur
and authoritarianism isolated him from the people and their
complaints. Despite all the talk of Nkrumah's charisma over
so many years, people joyfully knocked down his statues
after he fell. There is danger that Mobutu is worrying about

only the facade of unity—adulation for the leader—and not
about the government services in the bush that will really
make a peasant hundreds of miles away believe that the
Congo is important.

Neglect, in fact, is the hallmark of the new Congo. In
the Eastern Congo, the area hurt most by the incessant re-
bellions of the first years, the government has done almost
nothing to reactivate agriculture or maintain the roads
needed to take food to markets.

NIGERIA: THE JUICY MORSEL [3]

As I stood in one corner of that vast tumult waiting for the
arrival of the Minister I felt intense bitterness welling up in my
heart. Here were silly, ignorant villagers dancing themselves lame
and waiting to blow off their gunpowder in honor of one of those
who had started the country off down the slopes of inflation. I
wished for a miracle, for a voice of thunder, to hush this ridiculous
festival and tell the poor contemptible people one or two truths.
But of course it would be quite useless. They were not only ignorant but cynical. Tell them that this man had used his position
to enrich himself and they would ask you—as my father did—if
you thought that a sensible man would spit out the juicy morsel
that good fortune had placed in his mouth.—Chinua Achebe, *A
Man of the People*

When, in 1914, Nigeria was constituted a single political
unit, the only bond of political unity was the person of
Lugard, the governor general. The only occasions on which
the higher officials of two separate bureaucracies, one in the
north, and the other in the south, could meet was at the
annual session of the Legislative Council in Lagos. For all
the formal act of unification, Nigeria was still run as two
colonies. Two distinct administrative centers of power were
built: one in Kaduna, the other in Lagos. A frequently
heard quip was that if all the Africans were to leave Nigeria,
the southern and northern administrations could go to war.

[3] From *Power in Africa,* by Ruth First, South African exile who lives in
London and travels extensively through Africa. Penguin African Library. Baltimore, Maryland. '72. p 144-59. Copyright © 1970 by Ruth First. Reprinted
by permission of Pantheon Books/Division of Random House, Inc.

In administration, in land policy, in a dozen different fields of colonial government, the administration reinforced not the unity of the colony, but the differences between north and south. For a quarter of a century, from 1922 to 1947, there was no representative political structure of any sort that brought the regions together. . . .

Unequal Heirs

The 1958 Constitutional Conference rocked this pre-independence balance of control between south and north. With Nigeria about to be launched towards independence, the old British pledge to protect the North—and use it as ballast for conservatism in the old state—had to be honored. The federal parliament, it was laid down, would be elected on the basis of the population figures. The north, with over half Nigeria's population, was thus guaranteed cast-iron political domination of the country.

Thus, at the time of independence, two heirs shared the estate, but they were unequally treated in the will. The favored child was the traditional ruling oligarchy of the north; the less favored, the southern business-political class. The constitutional allocation of power . . . weighted political control in favor of the numerically preponderant, more backward north; in favor of the rural, tied peasantry, as against the urban wage earners. The region that had achieved self-government last, and had even tried to hold back the date of independence, emerged as the controlling force of the most populous independent state in Africa.

This major divide between south and north—the first, commercially competitive and beginning to industrialize; the second, under the control of an agrarian oligarchy—looked like possessing the potential of an American civil war. But the ultimate contradiction implicit in the economic cleavage did not become determinant in Nigerian politics. The north-south antagonism glimmered and flared, subsided and flamed again from time to time; but the polarities did not remain constant. East, west and north threw up fresh

combinations and conflicts. When the political system broke
down altogether over the sharing of spoils, and when civil
war finally came, it was not between north and south, but
followed a different lineup of forces. This lineup may well
have looked unlikely from the preindependence viewpoint;
but it developed with cruel logic across six years, in which
the political classes of the three regions ground the faces of
their competitors in order to get control of the federation. . . .

Constitutionalism Under Siege

Constitutionalism, the idol of the independence generation of politicians, cracked on its pedestal only two years
after the inauguration of independence, when the federal
government used its control of the center to crush an opposition regional government. A state of emergency was ar-
bitrarily imposed though no emergency existed. And when,
a few years later, again in the west, an emergency did, patently, exist, the federal government refused to invoke its
constitutional powers against the minority government that
was its political ally, even though that government had been
reduced to rule by open violence. . . .

Crisis of Confidence

Nowhere outside the west did the political crisis reach
such a total breakdown of civil government; but throughout
Nigeria there was a profound disgust with politicians and
politics. In the towns, there was a groundswell of popular
discontent. Laborer and young professional were equally
disillusioned with independence. In six years, Nigeria's political class had staggered drunkenly through a series of crises,
each more damaging than the last, using ballot box, parliamentary speech, bribery, nepotism and, where required,
thuggery, in the struggle for power. In the beginning, they
had been obsessed with constitutional form and legal nicety;
then, when occasion demanded, they had scrapped them
outright. Burdened with a constitutional form that was

faulty and unworkable, the political class had strained it to snapping point. No amount of rearranging could restore the form, only a fundamental reappraisal of national needs, and a different generation of political leaders to try to meet them. But national needs were the last thing that the politicians considered. They built a mass following to win elections, then abandoned their electorates as they devoted themselves to their bank balances and their businesses. Corruption was not backdoor and furtive, but flaunted. Big men, men of power, lived on an extravagant scale. For a while, their communities enjoyed the reflected glory and whatever amenities their big men secured for them. But six years of fiddling the coffers to subsidize big men and their parties for the contest of power had wasted the country's economic resources, and the general benefits were drying up even in the favored areas.

Dividing the Spoils

At the bottom of the Nigerian political crisis was the quarrel over spoils. And this took place at two levels. The first was the rivalry of the regions, which competed against each other for a larger share of the federal revenue, and of the export trade; over the location of industries and the allocations of development capital. Federal politics had turned out to be the politics of northern domination; federal economics turned out to be the economics of northern development. In the Six Year Development Plan, the bulk of federal development spending is being concentrated in the north. When it came to the proposed iron and steel industry for Nigeria, the whole project was held up because the north would not agree to site it in the east, the location recommended by a feasibility study. In the end, three plants were proposed: one for the north, another for the east, and a third one for the west. None has yet been built.

On the seond level of the quarrel, there was competition —often called tribalism—for jobs, for promotion, for vice chancellorships of universities and chairmanships of corporations. In the beginning, the competition was fought out between westerners (the Yoruba) and easterners (mainly the Ibo) in the southern labor market, professions and public service. Nigerianization and the departure of expatriate officials produced a great spate of openings, but also fierce squabbles. The years just before independence had been boom years; but when commodity prices, especially that of cocoa, began to fall on the world market, and foreign capital did not arrive in the quantities anticipated, the supply of jobs began to dry up, and the elites, the school-leavers, the unemployed and the newcomers to the towns fought desperately for what there was. By the early 1960s, urban unemployment in the south was almost 30 percent; one in ten of the pupils who held a secondary-school certificate could not find work; and it was estimated that by 1968 there would be 1,000 unemployed university graduates in the area. Northerners, once insulated in their own system, began to assert their claims to the plums in federal government and employment. Three streams of competitors—excluding minority groups, which were permitted no distinct identity—used their political and community leverage to promote their own interests.

A job affected more than the applicant and his immediate family. Each post, especially the higher ones, benefited a host of kinsmen, a local community, a region. A dispute over a university vice chancellorship in Lagos, or Ibadan, became an interracial dispute. Politics were organized on a regional basis, and politics contrived economic opportunities. Even when the connection was not so intimate, the habit of ganging-up by region became virtually endemic, except in small uninfluential pockets of the society. The politicians had produced no ideology of national unity which would interpret conflict in social or class terms; and the structure of Nigeria at independence filtered all contests into regional, and so inevitably, ethnic or communal, channels.

THE SUDAN: THE NORTH-SOUTH SPLIT [4]

Physically, culturally, and ethnically the Republic of the Sudan is a microcosm of Africa. Its achievements, problems, and potentialities are in many respects typical of those of other African or Afro-Asian countries—particularly the belt of Sudanic states which runs across the continent from the Horn and the Red Sea in the east to the Atlantic Ocean in the west. Thus, like the great majority of Afro-Asian countries, the Sudan has been subjected to alien rule for considerable periods during its modern history; its existing boundaries, administrative institutions, and cultural outlook have been largely molded by its colonial masters; it developed a nationalist movement whose primary objective was the achievement of independence; and, since the fulfillment of that objective, it has been faced with a host of problems, chief amongst which is the erosion of nationalism, in the sense of loyalty to the homeland as a whole, and the resurgence or development of a variety of particularistic tendencies, loyalty to which has in some cases equaled or even surpassed loyalty to the nationalism under whose banner independence was won.

In at least one respect, however, the Sudan is unique among African countries and differs from even those Sudanic states which it resembles most: it is at one and the same time both African and Arab, the combination being present —especially in the six northern provinces—to a degree and in a manner which are not paralleled in any other country....

The termination of the Southern Policy . . . [introduced in the 1920s with the intention of eliminating Islam and the Arabic language and culture from the southern provinces and substituting tribal customs, Christianity, and the English language] was a great victory for the Sudanese nationalists, who . . . were unanimously opposed to it. . . . But the

[4] From "Arabism, Africanism, and Self-Identification in the Sudan," by Muddathir 'Abd al-Rahim, former head of the department of political science, University of Khartoum; currently, visiting professor, Makerere University College, Kampala. *Journal of Modern African Studies.* 8:233-9. Jl. '70. Reprinted by permission of the publishers, Cambridge University Press.

southern Sudanese, who emerged after the removal of the restrictions of the Southern Policy in 1946 and who, two years later, made their debut in national politics as members of the legislative assembly, were naturally very much the product of Southern Policy. This had had the effect of almost completely eliminating the cultural and religious bonds which had previously existed between the northern and southern provinces. Under the influence of this policy, furthermore, many southerners, especially those who had been to mission schools as distinct from tribal chiefs and elders, had been imbued with a spirit, not only of strong local patriotism, but of bitter hostility towards their northern compatriots. . . .

Many southern Sudanese—mostly graduates of Christian missionary schools—came to regard themselves as a different people or "nation" from the northerners and, as such, believed that they should have their own independent state; if some link with the northern Sudan had to be maintained, they felt it should be in the form of a weak federal, or confederal, arrangement. Exasperated by the length and intensity of the debate over the rights and the wrongs of the subject, some northerners, including several who have held or now hold responsible government posts, have come to similar conclusions; they argue, in addition, that the southern provinces are a "drag" or a liability on the north, and advocate that the south should be severed from the main body of the country at the earliest possible opportunity and be given the independent status which some southerners at any rate say that they wish to have.

"Arabism" and "Africanism"

These views (whatever their merits) are ultimately based on the differences between the northern and southern provinces, which are often summarized in the by now stereotyped statement that the northern Sudan is predominantly Muslim and Arab, while the southern Sudan is African and mainly pagan or Christian: that the two, therefore, are separate entities and cannot, in any shape or form, constitute a single state. . . . Thus "Arabism" is normally equated with the north while "Africanism" is used with reference to the south; and the terms are popularly regarded as having a racial content and being mutually exclusive.

In fact, however, Arabism, which is a basic attribute of the majority of the population of the Sudan and of many other African countries, is not a racial bond which unites the members of a certain ethnic group. It is a cultural, linguistic, and nonracial link that binds together numerous races—black, white, and brown. Had Arabism been anything else but this, most modern Arabs, both African and Asian, including the entire population of the northern Sudan, would cease to be Arab at all. And just as Arabism is a cultural and nonracial bond, so Africanism is a geographical, political, and cultural—but nonracial—link which binds together the various peoples of Africa irrespective of differences of race, color, or language. Hence the close association between Arabism and Africanism, not only within the bounds of Africa itself but on interregional and international levels as well.

In the Sudan, which, as already noted, is a microcosm of Africa with all its physical, racial, and cultural diversities, Arabism and Africanism have become so completely merged in the northern provinces that it is impossible to distinguish between the two, even from the most abstract point of view; the great majority of the population rightly feel that they are Arab and African at the same time, to an equal degree, and without any sense of tension or contradiction. The fact that they are predominantly Muslim and Arab does indeed distinguish the northern Sudanese from their southern compatriots, who are mainly pagan and, to a much lesser extent, either Christian or Muslim; but it does not mean that they are not African. As the only region in the continent—and indeed the world—in which the physical, racial, and cultural diversities of Africa as a whole are not merely represented but synthesized into a unique and unparalleled entity, the

northern Sudan may in fact be described as more representative of Africa as a whole than any other country or region,
including the southern Sudan.

Plea for Unity

Nevertheless, the northern Sudan differs from the south
in that it is predominantly Muslim and Arab, while the latter is mainly pagan and only to a much lesser extent either
Muslim or Christian. This, though it may correctly be regarded as an adequate ground for claiming a special status
for the south within the framework of a united Sudan, does
not constitute a sound argument for the splitting of the
Sudan into two independent sovereign states. For the modern state, especially in Africa, is not and could not be found-
ed on religious, racial, or even cultural homogeneity. It is
based, above all, on the community of interests and objectives of peoples who, different though they may be in certain
respects, have met across continental and not merely tribal
or regional boundaries. In the present age Africa, of which
the Sudan constitutes an integral part and a uniquely representative cross-section, is moving towards unity and close
association rather than in the direction of separation and
Balkanization. Viewed against this background, the splitting
of the Sudan into two (or more probably, in that case,
several) parts would not only be unnecessary and undesirable as a matter of principle; it would also have serious
practical repercussions on Africa as a whole, and—in an age
when the race question is becoming of increasingly great
importance—it might, from a worldwide point of view, be
a most tragic event.

INDIA, PAKISTAN AND BANGLADESH [5]

A drastic reordering of the pattern of power in South
Asia has taken place, directly affecting the future of more

[5] From "The New Order in South Asia," by Norman D. Palmer, professor
of political science and South Asian studies, University of Pennsylvania. *Orbis.*
15:1109-13+. Winter '72. Reprinted by permission.

than one fifth of the human race. As a result of what might be termed the second partition of the subcontinent, the political picture in South Asia has a wholly different complexion, and several new factors have been introduced into the Asian and the larger international scene. The Pakistan that had existed since 1947 has disappeared. In its place is a truncated remnant in West Pakistan, with some 58 million people (less than half the population of the former state), an unstable government, a shaky internal situation, and an economy incapable of supporting the previous levels of military and political activity. India has clearly become the dominant South Asian power—a position its spokesmen claim is simply a consequence of "the natural balance" in the subcontinent. Under the determined leadership of Mrs. Indira Gandhi, . . . India is exhibiting a new assertiveness and self-reliance in domestic, regional and international affairs.

A new state—Bangladesh—has emerged in what was formerly East Pakistan (East Bengal). In demographic terms it is the world's eighth largest nation and the second largest Muslim state. Within little more than a year the people of this area suffered from the worst natural disaster [floods inundated 13,000 villages, leaving 500,000 homeless] and perhaps the second worst manmade disaster (second only to Hitler's extermination of the Jews) in the twentieth century. In December 1970, in the first nationwide general elections on the basis of direct adult franchise in the history of Pakistan, they had voted overwhelmingly for a single party, the Awami League, led by Sheikh Mujibur Rahman and dedicated to an extreme degree of autonomy for the east wing of the country. When negotiations between their leader and President Yahya Khan and Z. A. Bhutto, whose Pakistan People's Party had won a majority of the votes in West Pakistan, broke down, they resorted to violence. After March 25, 1971, when Yahya Khan ordered the armed forces, most of whom were West Pakistanis, to use whatever degree of force was necessary to coerce them, their demands escalated in favor of complete independence. This objective was achieved after a bloody civil war between the Mukti Bahini and other champions of an independent Bangladesh, on the one hand, and the Pakistani armed forces, aided by some collaborators, mostly Behari Muslims, on the other. During the conflict some one million people were slaughtered and ten million more fled into India as refugees. Undoubtedly the civil war would have gone on for a much longer time if the increased tension between India and Pakistan resulting from the crisis had not culminated in the two-week war of December 1971.

Thus Bangladesh is of tragic origin, the product of West Pakistani exploitation and ultimate repression, East Bengali resistance and civil war, and India's armed action.

India's Role

From the outset Indian sympathies were openly on the side of the East Pakistanis, and after March 25, 1971, they were vociferously expressed. A resolution introduced by Mrs. Gandhi and adopted unanimously by both houses of the Indian parliament on March 31 expressed "wholehearted sympathy and support" for the people of East Bengal, and called on the government of Pakistan "to put an end immediately to the systematic decimation of the people, which amounts to genocide."

India was affected by the tragic events in East Pakistan in innumerable ways. The spillover effects placed grave new strains on its political system, social structure and economy. Fortunately, the political system had been given new stability and direction as a result of the decisive victory in the fifth general elections, in March 1971, of the new Congress Party, led by Mrs. Gandhi. The economic outlook, while still by no means promising, seemed to be improving, and the threats to law and order, especially in the volatile state of West Bengal, seemed to be lessening. The influx of refugees from East Pakistan, mostly into the already depressed and troubled state of West Bengal, created serious problems.

Refugee relief became a well-nigh intolerable economic burden, especially since the international community provided amazingly little financial support. By December 1971, the refugees numbered around ten million, their flight marking one of the greatest such movements of "the century of the homeless man," and relief for them was costing India between two and three million dollars a day. Increasingly Indians voiced demands for military intervention, if necessary, to create conditions favorable for the return of the refugees to their homes. The feeling was widespread that the actions of the Pakistani armed forces in East Pakistan and the failure of the international community to come to India's aid in supporting the refugees or to bring an end to the "genocide" had left New Delhi with no option except a resort to force.

The Pakistan government repeatedly charged India with "deliberate and blatant interference" in its internal affairs, and with sustained efforts "to undermine the solidarity and national integrity of Pakistan." It insisted that it had been compelled to use force to preserve the integrity of the nation against a group of "miscreants and antistate people" in East Pakistan, egged on by Indian agents and supported from Indian territory. Even though a large number of foreign correspondents, United Nations officials and other outside observers generally corroborated the Indian figures, it maintained that India was deliberately exaggerating the extent of the casualties in East Pakistan and the number of refugees who had fled into India. President Yahya Khan warned that war was inevitable unless India ceased to "intervene" in Pakistan's "internal affairs."

In all probability any prospects for holding Pakistan together ended on the night of March 25, 1971, when the Pakistan army was loosed with ruthless fury on the people of the eastern wing. It may even be argued that Pakistan was doomed from the beginning because of the disparities and frictions between the two wings and the absence of the cement of nationhood. The growing estrangement between east and west was dramatized and polarized in the elections of December 1970 and the abortive negotiations among Yahya Khan, Sheikh Mujibur Rahman and Z. A. Bhutto in the early weeks of 1971. Certainly the increased tensions between India and Pakistan after March 25, and Indian behavior under a determined leader supported by a people who suddenly seemed to have turned from "doves" into "hawks," made the hope of preserving Pakistan as a unified nation unrealistic.

As in a Greek tragedy, the two unfriendly neighbors drifted inexorably toward armed conflict which neither wanted or could afford. The drama became a classic case of escalation leading to a point of no return. Efforts of the United Nations, the United States, the Soviet Union and other members of the international community to avert the impending clash were pathetically halfhearted and ineffective; however well intentioned they were, they showed little understanding of the nature of the developments in East Pakistan and in South Asia generally, the basic causes of the crisis, or the significance of the changes that were taking place. A day after the war broke out the *Times of India* declared editorially:

There will be no dearth of advice to India from all kind of quarters. But men who have kept quiet in the face of the massacre of over half a million men, women and children and the expulsion of another ten million people from their homes have no moral right to advise this country, specially after the Pakistani aggression. New Delhi has given them long enough time to defuse the crisis in the subcontinent by ending the military occupation of East Bengal. It is under no obligation to listen to them now that the battle is joined.

Pakistan Divided

War came to South Asia, for the third time since 1947, on the evening of December 3, 1971, when Pakistani planes launched simultaneous attacks on airfields in west and northwest India. New Delhi promptly recognized Bangladesh as an independent sovereign nation and ordered Indian troops into the area. Within two weeks the Indians, in cooperation with the Mukti Bahini, forced the nearly 100,000 Pakistani troops in the east to surrender unconditionally, and representatives of Bangladesh moved from Calcutta to Dacca. On the western front Indian forces resisted Pakistani attacks, especially in the Chhamb sector of Jammu and Kashmir where the hardest battles of the war were fought, undertook some probes into Pakistani territory, neutralized the Pakistan air force, and carried out essentially a holding operation. The Indian navy played a significant role in two daring raids on Karachi harbor, sinking two of Pakistan's four submarines (one of which was "on loan" from the United States), and effectively interdicting the access routes by sea to both West and East Pakistan. When the Pakistani forces in East Bengal surrendered, India proclaimed a unilateral cease-fire on the western front on the evening of December 16. Yahya Khan, in a radio broadcast, charging that India was determined to dismember Pakistan and had "expansionist and imperialist designs," pledged that "our armed forces will not rest content until we throw the enemy out of our borders. . . . The *jihad* [holy war] against the treacherous enemy . . . will continue till victory is ours." But twenty-four hours later he announced acceptance of a cease-fire, and the war was over.

On December 19 Yahya Khan, who had been the strong man of Pakistan since the abrupt end of Ayub Khan's long rule (October 1958 to March 1969), was forced to resign, apparently on the decision of Pakistan's top military leaders. Z. A. Bhutto succeeded him as president and martial law administrator. While Bhutto promised, in a rambling and emotional radio address, not to rest until Pakistan was reunited and the military defeat by India was avenged, it was clear that the western remnant of the country lacked the capability to achieve either objective. Indeed, Bhutto's own political future, and the future of West Pakistan as a single national entity, were in jeopardy. A central question in South Asia today is whether West Pakistanis, under the leadership of Bhutto or his successors, can recover from the traumatic shock of the country's breakup and military defeat, adjust themselves to the unpleasant realities of a lesser role in South Asia and world affairs, and concentrate on the politics and economics of national survival.

Bangladesh, with more than seventy million people in a naturally fertile but small and underdeveloped area, has been inaugurated with great *élan,* strong support from India, and good prospects of recognition and aid from many other countries and international agencies. In the long run, however, the present euphoric relations between India and Bangladesh will have to give way to more prosaic and less intimate contacts. India, hampered by limited resources and its own serious economic problems, will not be able to provide the new state with the kind of long-range assistance it must have if it is to survive. Any attempt to guide the destinies of Bangladesh too directly may provoke charges of Indian imperialism in the nation New Delhi helped to create. With the exception of Sheikh Mujibur Rahman, who was imprisoned in West Pakistan during the entire course of the East Bengal crisis, from March 25, 1971, to early January 1972, the leaders of Bangladesh are relatively unknown and untried. If they cannot build a new polity from scratch, they will probably be thrust aside and more radical leaders —perhaps of a Maoist type—may take over and try to turn the proclaimed democratic, secular and Socialist state into a people's republic of an all-too-familiar type. . . .

The Outlook

The immediate effects of the crisis are crystal clear. A new order of power has emerged in South Asia. India has assumed a more dominant position and cannot now be effectively challenged by any other state of the region. The numerically large but economically weak new nation created in what was East Pakistan is heavily dependent on India for its continued survival. This may lead to various kinds of cooperative political and economic policies—and perhaps in time to frictions and strains. Certainly, in spite of proclamations by Bangladesh and Indian spokesmen, the new nation will need extensive outside contacts and assistance if it is to cope with its basic problems of survival and development. The balance of forces within it, as well as the quality of its leadership, is quite uncertain. Pakistan, reduced to what was West Pakistan, is now only the third largest state in South Asia. It will either waste its limited resources on military and other commitments which it cannot long maintain or, perforce, make painful readjustments to the stark realities of the new order. It may not be able to survive the coming ordeals. If it does, it will be a new Pakistan, in more than a territorial sense. Much will depend on evolving relations among the new India, the new Pakistan and the new Bangladesh. If antagonisms continue, the prospects for a happier era in South Asia will be dim. If patterns of cooperation and cordial relations develop, the outlook will greatly improve. In any event, South Asia will almost certainly remain a troubled area of both hope and danger for some time to come.

TRIBAL POLITICS HARASS KENYA [6]

Before the murder of Tom Mboya in July 1969, Kenya politicians could mute and obscure their country's tribal tensions. The tensions, of course, were always there, straining the fragile unity of the new country, but they did not pervade every side of political life. Personal rivalry counted; so did ideology. The assassination changed all that.

For more than a year, Kenya was torn by a dangerous and blatant tribal conflict that colored all political activity. In a sense, this only followed what had happened elsewhere in Africa, where crisis invariably heightens tribal hatreds and suspicions. The results, as Nigeria showed, can be terrifying. But Kenya is not another Nigeria. In recent months, the fury has diminished, giving Kenya a time of calm to deal

[6] From article by Stanley Meisler, Africa correspondent of the Los Angeles *Times. Foreign Affairs*. 49:111-16. O. '70. Excerpted by permission from *Foreign Affairs*, October 1970. Copyright © 1970 by the Council on Foreign Relations, Inc., New York.

with its tribal problems. Its future depends on whether its
politicians learn to do so.

At stake is a land of 10.5 million people led by pragmatic
men who have nursed the old white settler economy so well
that Kenya has one of the highest economic growth rates in
black Africa. No other black African country has anything
to compare with its fertile soil and energetic farmers. Its
wildlife and incredible and varied beauty have made it the
tourist center of black Africa. But all this is threatened by
the instability inherent in tribalism.

Before analyzing the tribal problem, it makes sense to
recount the excited political events of the country since the
death of Mboya. They rushed on Kenya in a breathless way,
moving so swiftly that they seemed part of a novel or a film
rather than a real political story. Stark, dramatic events
sometimes have a way of oversimplifying the complexities
of a political and social problem. In this case, however, they
helped to reveal the intensity and urgency of the problem,
demonstrating how tribalism can suddenly take hold of an
African country and blot out all else.

Background

Mboya, the Minister for Economic Planning and Development, was gunned down by an assassin on a crowded
shopping street in downtown Nairobi. Unlike almost all
other politicians in Africa, Mboya had never appealed to
tribal chauvinism. He was an urban man who had come to
power through the labor unions. In parliament, he represented a Nairobi district, where few of the voters came from
his Luo tribe.

Mboya had never had the support of most of the Luos,
the second largest tribe in Kenya with 1.3 million people.
The majority were behind Oginga Odinga, a Luo tribal
elder who was the leader of the leftist opposition party, the
Kenya People's Union (KPU), a former vice president of
the country, and a bitter personal enemy of Mboya. A large
minority, however, joined Mboya in supporting the govern-

ment of President Jomo Kenyatta, a leader of the Kikuyu tribe, the largest in Kenya with 2 million people. As long as the Luos divided this way, Kenya politics could stay above tribal conflict.

But the assassination united the Luos behind Odinga. The Luos assumed immediately that the Kikuyus, who dominated the government and were the best-educated people in Kenya, had murdered Mboya. In death, Mboya became a great tribal hero to the Luos. Since they believed the Kikuyus in government had murdered him, they decided they must now support the Luo leader who was a proven enemy of that Kikuyu government. The years when Odinga schemed against Mboya were forgotten.

The Luos went on an emotional rampage. They stoned and threw shoes at the Mercedes of President Kenyatta while he drove to the memorial services for Mboya at the Roman Catholic cathedral in Nairobi. At the burial by the family home on Rusinga island in Lake Victoria, Luos chanted, "War with the Kikuyus." A medicine man cursed, "May the wombs of all Kikuyu women dry up." "Where is Jomo Kenyatta?" another mourner shouted. "If he were here, even if he were guarded by one hundred thousand soldiers, I would kill him." The chanting also revealed the new political alignment. "Tom, why did you join with them?" several wailed by the coffin. Another mourner chanted by the graveside, "When things get worse, there is only one man who can save us. That is Jaramogi (Odinga's Luo title). Where is he? I am looking for him in the crowd." When Odinga did show up, he was lifted in the air and carried around the grave. . . .

Oathing

The fury and unity of the Luos after the death of Mboya frightened the Kikuyus. When threatened in the past, the Kikuyus have often resorted to oaths as a way of strengthening themselves. They had done so during Mau Mau days when they wanted to unite against the British colonial government and the white settlers. In those days the mysterious and bestial nature of the oaths had shocked both other tribes and outsiders. The Kikuyus went back to oathing this time and shocked outsiders and other tribes again.

In an oathing ceremony, Kikuyus, after drinking goat's blood or undergoing some other ritual, swear allegiance to a tribal cause. Whether they oathe voluntarily or are forced to take part, many Kikuyus believe they will be struck dead by sacred spirits if they break the pledge. In this case, according to reports in parliament, the Kikuyus would stand naked in a dark room in a house on the grounds of the home of President Kenyatta and take an oath that they would never allow the flag of Kenya to leave the "house of Mumbi," as Kikuyus call their tribe. Other tribes believed this meant that the Kikuyus wanted to keep the presidency indefinitely and dominate them forever. The other tribes were angered and frightened even more by the seeming acquiescence of Kenyatta.

In October 1969, with elections only a few weeks away, Kenyatta decided to show the country that he was still its national leader. He drove to Kisumu, the main town of Luo land, to dedicate a Russian-built hospital there. From the first, he was received with anger. Luos held up signs asking, "Where's Tom?" Some threw stones. Many shouted the slogan of Odinga's opposition party. This enraged Kenyatta. In Swahili, he shouted at the crowd at the hospital, "I can assure you, my brothers, that anybody who brings trouble . . . will be taught to know that Kenya has a government." He cursed at his opponents and boasted, "We are going to crush you into flour." The crowds grew disorderly again after the speech. As the president's motorcade drove out of town, the Luos threw rocks and surged toward the car of the president. This panicked the bodyguard, and they fired into the crowd. The toll was eleven dead and many wounded.

Kenyatta blamed Odinga for both the insults and the carnage. He banned the opposition party and detained Odinga and the other seven opposition members of parliament. With their two leaders gone, the Luos dropped to the low point of their fortunes. On the eve of elections, the party that most represented them was banned.

Calm Returns

This was probably the most critical moment in Kenya's history since independence. The plight of the Luos seemed desperate. To outsiders, it appeared that Kenyatta and the Kikuyus had gone too far. The horror of Nigeria was on everyone's mind, and many waited for an explosion. Instead, Kenya dropped into a calm. It is not exactly clear why this happened, but several reasons can be suggested.

First, Africans live in tribal societies that respect authority. Kenyatta asserted his authority in an uncompromising way and made it clear he would continue to do so. This shocked the Luos and sobered their rage. They withdrew like a child slapped by an angry father. Second, the Luos, though emotional, have a tribal personality that allows them to accept adversity in a fatalistic way. Their grievances were bitter, but this did not provoke them into acts of revenge. Instead, they bemoaned their fate. Third, they realized how little they could do. Western Kenya was not Eastern Nigeria. Unlike the grieving Ibos, the Luos did not have a government or even a radio to rally the people. In centralized Kenya, these instruments of secession belonged to Kenyatta in Nairobi. The Luos could not have broken away even if they had wanted to.

Finally, the detention of Odinga allowed a group of younger, better educated and more moderate Luo leaders to come forward. They had long felt that Odinga was leading his people astray. In their view, the Luos needed to align themselves with the government, not to fight it. The young men counseled patience.

The government helped the calm by allowing a remarkable election in December 1969. Ironically, with only one party, the election turned out to be far more democratic than it probably would have been with two. The election

became a free-for-all primary within the ruling party much
like the old statewide democratic primaries in the American
South. Anyone could vote in it, even members of the banned
opposition party. In addition, the government allowed Mrs.
Grace Onyango, a lieutenant of Odinga in the banned party,
to stand for office in the government primary. It was a
shrewd political move by Kenyatta. The election became a
way for all peoples of Kenya, whether Luo or not, to demonstrate their grievances and hostilities. They defeated
eighty-two incumbent members of parliament, including five
ministers. In one of the most sweeping turnovers in any
African election, the voters sent newcomers into two thirds
of the seats in parliament....

The government chose not to interpret the election as
a vote of no confidence or as an expression of hostility to
Kikuyu dominance. Spokesmen for the government noted
ingenuously that everyone had run on the same party platform and therefore could be considered supporters of the
government. Moreover, the primary machinery did not allow
an opponent for Kenyatta as president. He was reelected
automatically.

The results, however, did lay bare the disquieting tribal
problems of Kenya....

The government ... was probably right in not panicking
over the results. The election, in a sense, had given Kenya
a reprieve. There was a feeling that a fresh start was now
possible. Kenya now had a chance to deal with its awesome
tribal problem without crisis; Kenya had time and calm.

BURUNDI: SLAUGHTER OF THE HUTUS [7]

Africa has witnessed more than its share of tragedies in
recent years—the chaos in the Congo, the long civil war in
the Sudan, the bloody Biafran seccession. But for sheer savagery, nothing surpassed the recent outburst of tribal
hatred in Burundi, a land of beautiful green hills tucked

[7] Article entitled "Slaughter of the Hutus." *Newsweek.* 79:39-40. Je. 26,
'72. Copyright Newsweek, Inc. 1972, reprinted by permission.

away between Zaïre (formerly the Congo) and Tanzania. The slaughter there began two months ago [April 1972] when members of the Bahutu tribe, which composes 85 percent of the 3.6 million population, rose up against their towering, aristocratic Watutsi overlords. By last week, the murderous conflict had apparently come to an end with the "Tutsi" still in control, and more than 100,000 "Hutu" men, women and children the victims of calculated genocide.

Rebel Attack

The violence erupted April 29 when the Hutu launched a countrywide attack against the Tutsi-led government of President Michel Micombero, a swashbuckling figure who sports a sweeping mustache and sideburns. The rebels, some of whom had secretly trained across the border in Tanzania, were well armed and might have succeeded if they had taken the capital of Bujumbura. But the alarm was raised when a rebel band stopped at a filling station to buy gasoline for their Molotov cocktails and chopped off the attendant's fingers when he demanded payment. This brought government troops to the scene, and a rebel attack, scheduled for several hours later, was averted. Even so, there were some desperate hours for the Tutsis. In the countryside, the Hutu rebels mercilessly slaughtered pregnant Tutsi women, then disemboweled them so that no Tutsi fetus might survive. The widow of one Tutsi police captain was forced to look on in horror as the Hutu beheaded her three children, disemboweled her husband and stuffed the children's heads into his stomach. Then she was raped repeatedly and left for dead.

It took nearly two weeks for the Burundi government, aided by troops flown in from Zaïre, to bring the situation under control. But once the Tutsis felt safe from extermination, they began to exact a terrible revenge. All over the country, terrified Hutus were herded together by soldiers and government officials, then bayoneted, shot or beaten to death. Then, their bodies were piled high in lorries and taken off at night to mass graves in the countryside.

But the Tutsi vengeance went far beyond mere eye-for-an-eye retribution. In fact, the Micombero government embarked on nothing less than the deliberate and systematic slaughter of every Hutu with any education or leadership ability. "They began at the top with Hutu ministers in the government and senior officials in the administration," said one Western diplomat. "They had lists of educated Hutus and went from place to place picking them out by name, slowly working their way downward." Perhaps the heaviest blow fell on Hutu schoolchildren, who were dragged out of their schools and taken away for slaughter. "They slaughtered the sons of educated Hutus," said one missionary, "to try to buy for themselves another generation of survival."

Curiously, the bloody events in Burundi elicited little outrage in black Africa. But . . . after protests from Pope Paul, Belgian Premier Gaston Eyskens and President Grégoire Kayibanda of neighboring Rwanda, Micombero reportedly called off the bloodletting. By then, an estimated 5,000 to 10,000 Tutsi and some 100,000 Hutus lay dead. And the blood bath had shattered any hope of building a viable multitribal state in Burundi. "Until this slaughter," said one foreign resident in Bujumbura, "the Tutsi and Hutus were very gradually beginning to work alongside each other. Now the violence has canceled out everything that had been accomplished."

III. POLITICAL STABILITY: ELUSIVE GOAL

EDITOR'S INTRODUCTION

The cherished dream, held by many political optimists on the eve of independence, that colonial rule would be replaced by free democracies has not been fulfilled. Democracy today is the exception, and government by a single party or a military dictatorship the rule. In the first two selections in this section, Fred R. von der Mehden, professor of political science at Rice University, traces the influence of the colonial heritage and the preparation—or lack of it—for self-government on the political institutions of the new nations.

The rise and decline of the single party in Africa is related by L. Gray Cowan, an authority on Africa. One single-party state that is still alive and well and appears to be functioning effectively is Tanzania.

The military are a relatively new phenomenon on the political scene in many countries. Professor von der Mehden explains what prompts the military to get into politics, Brookings Senior Fellow Ernest W. Lefever describes the army's debut on the African stage, and Ruth First then gives her opinion as to why the military coup has proved to be so contagious.

The new military leaders are frequently as different one from the other as they are from the civilians they supplanted. Two examples are Uganda's unpredictable General Amin, whose portrait is sketched by the New York *Times* correspondent Charles Mohr, and Libya's ascetic Colonel Kaddafi, described by *Newsweek*'s Loren Jenkins.

Among the few leaders who have managed to ride out the political storms of the postindependence era is North

Korea's Kim. His staying power as head of one of a handful of Communist nations that emerged after World War II is analyzed by the Toronto *Star's* Mark Gayn.

Although the survival rate of the democracies on the whole has been poor, there are exceptions. One is India. Indian journalist Krishan Bhatia assesses India's political prospects. The outlook for another democracy, the Philippines, is uncertain since the imposition of martial law in 1972. The *Wall Street Journal's* Peter R. Kann looks at the meaning behind President Marcos' action.

Rooting out corruption was one of President Marcos' stated objectives, and indeed corruption has frequently been cited to justify resort to military rule in recent years. The final selections look at two aspects of the problem. Corruption in Indonesia is dissected by Willard A. Hanna of the American Universities Field Staff, and University of Maryland Professor Herbert H. Werlin looks at Ghana's record.

GOVERNMENT: THE COLONIAL HERITAGE [1]

Political institutions and processes are not shaped by colonial administration alone; nevertheless, general patterns have emerged under the different colonial systems. Two factors are significant: the level of political stability, as based upon the number of revolutions or major coups (whether successful or not) to which the new nation has been subjected; and the type of government established after independence, on the basis of party system and extra-constitutional control of the government (primarily military takeover or suspension of democratic institutions).

Several interesting points . . . [can be charted]. Instability, as defined by the incidence of attempted or successful

[1] From *Politics of the Developing Nations*, by Fred R. von der Mehden, professor of political science, Rice University. 2d ed. Prentice-Hall. '69. p 18-21. Copyright © 1969 by Prentice-Hall, Inc., Englewood Cliffs, New Jersey. Reprinted by permission.

Chart: Postcolonial Revolutions and Coup Attempts
in Afro-Asia [as of 1969]

Colonial Power	Number of Colonies	Number (and Percentage) of Former Colonies Subjected to Revolutions or Coup Attempts
France	24	16 (67) [1]
United Kingdom	24	15 (62) [2]
Belgium	3	3 (100) [3]
United States	1	1 (100) [4]
Netherlands	1	1 (100) [5]
Independent States	11	10 (91) [6]

[1] Laos, South Vietnam, Syria, Lebanon, Senegal, Algeria, Togo, Dahomey, Mali, Cambodia, Central African Republic, Congo, Gabon, Morocco, Tunisia, Upper Volta

[2] Nigeria, Pakistan, Ceylon [Sri Lanka], Burma, Iraq, Jordan, Sudan, Tanzania (Zanzibar), Ghana, Kenya, Sierra Leone, Uganda, Singapore, Guyana

[3] Congo [Zaïre], Rwanda, Burundi

[4] Philippines

[5] Indonesia

[6] Thailand, Turkey, Liberia, Saudi Arabia, Yemen, Ethiopia, China, Korea, Iran, Egypt. Only those states which have been independent during the twentieth century are considered. Arabian sheikdoms and Himalayan kingdoms are not considered. Their inclusion would vastly increase the number of states with revolts, attempted and successful.

coups or revolution, can be correlated to the length of time a country has been independent. It should be noted that former British colonies, which show a higher percentage of instability, have been independent longer than most French colonies and thus have had more time in which to develop internal troubles. (Also, a number of those areas experiencing revolutions and coups—Lebanon, Syria, Iraq, Togo, and Jordan—were not colonies but were administered as mandates.) Only Liberia has not displayed this common tendency in recent years. One method of testing this correlation between time and instability might be to compare the level of stability in former colonies and mandates which have achieved their independence before 1958 with that of those which received theirs later.

These figures show an almost universal instability among countries which achieved independence before 1958.

Perhaps it would not be unfair to conclude that if the former colonial administrators intended to provide the foundations for peace and order, they were somewhat less than successful.

Postindependence Systems of Government: Afro-Asia

Extraconstitutional governments have also been common in former colonies which have been independent for longer periods of time. . . .

It is one of the ironies of postwar politics that France, often criticized for the instability and *immobilisme* of her multiparty system, should be the mother to so many one-party states. Of the twenty-four former French colonies and mandates now independent, thirteen have one-party-dominant systems. The major influence on the politics of former French colonies may have come from the French Left, to which so many postwar African leaders were drawn. The other irony is that the United Kingdom—the "Mother of Parliaments"—has tied France for the largest number of states with extraconstitutional governments and has spawned seven political systems in which parties play no effective role. In fact, of the Afro-Asian governments in which the military has led a successful coup, France and Britain hold equal honors with eight formerly controlled territories each. Again, this instability may arise from the fact that these states have been independent for relatively longer periods. The United States can, perhaps, claim some of the credit for the only independent Afro-Asian country with a democratic two-party system: the Philippines. [Martial law was declared by President Marcos in September 1972.—Ed.]

In conclusion, it cannot be stated that the colonial powers provided their colonies with the foundations for democratic systems similar to their own. It is almost as though the former colonies had consciously rejected the proffered model.

PREPARATION FOR SELF-GOVERNMENT: ADMINISTRATIVE VACUUM [2]

Colonial administration, with rare exceptions, was poor preparation for self-government. In most cases the period of training in modern administration and the time available to expand communications and to unite dissident groups was extremely short. The average period of colonialism for the African nations was only about seventy-five years. Also, until the twentieth century few colonial powers considered it their duty to prepare their colonies for independence. (Portugal still refuses to admit the idea.) Even after the colonial powers acknowledged their responsibility, numerous obstacles were posed by die-hard colonialists at home and in the field. The degree of "nativization" varied from colony to colony and among the various colonial systems, but many a report on "nativization" of the civil service noted the unwillingness of colonial officers to entrust responsibility to the native peoples. Toward the end of World War II, the French government asked its senior civil servants to provide the names of Africans capable of filling high posts. None was submitted. A British report on the Nigerianization of the civil service commented adversely on the attitude of senior civil servants toward the advancement of Africans to high posts. Where there existed a "proletariat" of lower-rank European civil servants, as in French Indo-China and the Dutch East Indies, the problem was even more difficult and training began even later.

Perhaps the most effective colonial power, in this respect, was the United States, which had largely nativized the civil service of the Philippines by the 1920s. The British also had a good record, although it varied greatly. For example, a comparatively good program was established in India and Ceylon, but nativization began much later in Ghana, Ni-

[2] From *Politics of the Developing Nations*, by Fred R. von der Mehden, professor of political science, Rice University. 2d ed. Prentice-Hall. '69. p 22-4. Copyright © 1969 by Prentice-Hall, Inc., Englewood Cliffs, New Jersey. Reprinted by permission.

geria, and Uganda, and still later in the former colonies of
Somalia, Lesotho, Tanzania, the former Rhodesias, and
Malawi.

The Case of Uganda

In Uganda, only five higher civil service posts were oc-
cupied by Africans in 1952 and fifty in 1958. It was hoped
that one quarter of the higher posts would be Africanized
by the time independence was achieved. The pace was so
slow that, some claimed, it would take twenty-five years before Uganda was 70 percent Africanized. Uganda—like so
many other states—became independent before her administrators were adequately trained, and personal and political
pressures caused the country to lose its trained foreigners.
(It was estimated that 60 percent of the European civil servants left the country by March 1963.) In an even more difficult position were Tanzania and Malawi. In Tanzania, only
700 of the 4889 senior staff positions had been Africanized
by late 1961, at which time there were in Malawi only thirty-
three natives educationally trained to take over the more
highly skilled posts. It was estimated that if the 1960-61 rate
of education in Malawi were maintained, there would be
only 120 properly trained personnel to fill these posts by
1971.

The French had achieved a very high percentage of Africanization at the lower levels (almost 100 percent in West
and Equatorial Africa by the mid-1950s), but a much lower
percentage in the middle levels (about 25 percent in West
Africa and 33 percent in Equatorial Africa), and they admitted very few Africans to top-level policymaking positions
(perhaps 6 percent in Equatorial Africa).

The Belgians entrusted no policymaking positions to
Africans until the very late 1950s. Native Congolese were
almost universally held to clerical positions and could not
rise above the rank of noncommissioned officer in the army.
(To discuss Africanization in the Spanish and Portuguese
colonies would be to give too much space to what has been
almost totally nonexistent.)

Inexperience Causes Administrative Problems

One aspect of this "too little too late" training was that the postindependence civil service suffered from a paucity of experienced officers at top levels. Where the Europeans refused to cooperate with the new nation (the French took everything—including office fixtures—from Guinea when that country refused to enter the French Community), or where Europeans were dismissed before nationals had been adequately trained (as in Indonesia), serious administrative problems arose. In a number of countries, the problem was further complicated by nationalist charges that the natives who had worked for the colonial civil service were tools of the imperialists or antinationalists and therefore not fit for higher positions. The most obvious examples of this situation occurred in Burma and Indonesia, where the colonial administrators had employed a high percentage of members of religious and ethnic minority groups in civil service positions.

Furthermore, many civil servants who did not suffer from the stigma of colonialism too often preferred to enter politics, leaving serious gaps in both central and provincial administration. (Provincial governments also lost able participants to national politics.) This was more natural in former French colonies, where the civil servant was not expected to remain aloof from politics. Thus, some new countries lost their trained civil service personnel while others—including almost all Afro-Asian states—attained independence with an insufficiently trained staff to back politicians who were often even less experienced.

Paternalism Also a Factor

A second factor of colonialism which led to later instability was the paternalistic attitude of the colonial powers. One commentator on the Dutch administration in the Indies called it a hothouse atmosphere. This charge could be made against others as well. The philosophy of "the white man's burden" had several serious effects on postcolonial stability and unity. Paternalism did not foster self-reliance in the native population. Even more serious, the postindependence native administrators often retained an aloofness and an air of *noblesse oblige* which was characteristic of the colonial period. A relationship based upon mutual trust and respect could not develop and too little consideration was given to popular beliefs by those who thought that they knew what was best for the people.

The practice of indirect rule, the unwillingness in certain cases to expand the use of the colonial or national language, and the disproportionate use of minority groups in government posts all led to postindependence conflicts and difficulties in communication which complicated efforts to establish stable government. In some areas, as in French West Africa, the colonial regime had replaced traditional local rulers with bureaucrats who could not command the traditional respect and authority based on local tribal, religious, or blood ties. To a certain extent, the colonial authorities were damned if they did maintain traditional rule (thus perpetuating parochial loyalties) and damned if they didn't.

THE RISE AND DECLINE OF THE SINGLE PARTY [3]

The most pervasive political phenomenon in the new states [of black Africa] since independence has been the rise and subsequent decline of the single political party, led by a charismatic leader who usually played a major role in the political agitation leading up to independence. With very few exceptions the single-party-dominant system has been the major element of the political structure. Even in Nigeria, where no single national party existed, the former three major regions each had its own single-party structure. The single party derived from the national mobilization which

[3] From *Black Africa: The Growing Pains of Independence*, pamphlet by L. Gray Cowan, dean of the Graduate School of Public Affairs, State University of New York at Albany. (Headline Series No 210) Foreign Policy Association. 345 E. 46th St. New York 10017. '72. p 6-8+. Copyright © 1972 by the Foreign Policy Association, Inc. Reprinted by permission.

was a necessary feature of the demand for independence; its continuation in the postindependence years was the result of the leaders' desire to retain personal power and the lack of a broad popular consensus on the rules by which the national political game was to be played. In most black African states the disparity between the rich and the poor was so wide, and the personal gains to be drawn from a position of political power were so great that once leadership had been achieved, there was strong disinclination to surrender it. Where political opposition existed there was always the threat that power would be seized by revolution, since there was little prospect of a change in political leadership by means of the electoral process. The party in power therefore tended to regard all opposition as a threat to its own position and, by implication, to the political independence of the nation. Indeed, given the actions of some opposition groups, there may well have been some justification for this view.

Those in power argued that the single party was necessary to accomplish the development of the country, that it subsumed within it all of the interests in the nation, and that, such was the urgency of the problems of social and economic transformation faced by the government, the luxury of parliamentary bickering over details could not be afforded. The fact that most single parties commanded at the outset the support of the vast majority of the population meant that there was little role for the opposition to play. By the time the single party in power had become unpopular, organized opposition was largely destroyed, either through imprisonment, exile of its leaders or manipulation of the electoral system.

Many leaders maintained that the single party permitted within its ranks full discussion of public issues and that, therefore, the party represented all shades of popular opinion. Such may well have been the case in the period immediately after independence, but as the leadership became increasingly preoccupied with problems of foreign policy or with the complex details of technological modernization, less and less time could be devoted to listening to the popular voice. The activities of government became ever more remote from the people, and the paternalism which had marked the colonial administrations again became evident. Members of the government became increasingly intolerant of criticism from any quarter, believing that all such criticism was motivated either by ideological disagreement or by the desire to overthrow those in power. It was claimed that only through the continuation in power of the single national party could political stability be maintained and planned economic development be carried out. It became increasingly evident, however, that the single party was no guarantee of stability; as opposition became more desperate in its attempts to secure a voice in government, there was constantly growing danger of political explosion.

The effectiveness of the single party as a stabilizing factor was further threatened by the growing emphasis in many countries on ethnic differentiation (often inaccurately referred to as tribalism). Loyalty to a particular ethnic group provided a built-in base of political power, and many nationalist leaders first came to prominence as leaders of an ethnic group. Governments were increasingly accused after independence of ethnic favoritism. In those countries (such as Nigeria) where large ethnic minorities were denied what they believed to be their rightful place in government and a proportionate share of power, there was a constant temptation to break away from the ruling group which, it was felt, tended to become the preserve of those identified ethnically with its leadership. Ethnicity played a substantial role in the Nigerian-Biafran conflict, although here, as elsewhere, ethnic groups also competed as economic interest groups in the modernizing effort.

The defects of the single-party system became more evident as popular enthusiasm for its cause waned in the years following independence. For the generation of young people who came to political maturity in the postindependence period, the earlier achievements of the leaders had become a matter of history and not of personal experience. They were inclined to evaluate the government in terms of its ability to satisfy their current expectations, rather than to regard the leadership as the founding fathers of the nation. The younger people did not agree with the political preference given to those who had been most active in the independence struggle; despite the universal African respect for age and experience, there was the feeling that some of the older militants did not fully understand the complex problems of modernization with which the younger men knew they must deal. With the rapid expansion of bureaucracies after independence the more responsible posts in the civil service were often filled by those who had been party members over a period of years. This meant that few posts were available for younger people who felt that they had better education than those now in office and who were still far from retirement age.

Despite its defects, however, the single-party system provided the mechanism for a reasonably satisfactory transition from the colonial administration to independent government. No government, however successful, could have been expected to maintain the degree of popular support over a period of time which the new nationalist-party governments enjoyed at the outset. In a few instances, where there prevailed a fortunate combination of circumstances involving the personality of the leader, ample internal resources for development and an available supply of technical assistance, such as in the Ivory Coast, the single party which came to power at independence has remained in office. In some other instances, the personality of the leader has been strong enough, as in Guinea, Tanzania and Senegal, to maintain control of the government, even in the face of popular dissatisfaction; but even in these instances the governments have not been immune from attempted overthrow. Where the military have been successful in overthrowing the leader, the party and its elaborate structure have vanished from

public view almost overnight. Ghana provides the classic
example of this with the disappearance of the Convention
People's party upon the overthrow of Kwame Nkrumah.

TANZANIA: SINGLE PARTY, MULTIPLE CHOICE [4]

In one of the single-party countries, Tanzania, experi-
ments have been tried in offering genuine choice within the
single-party structure for election of candidates in both local
and national elections. President Julius K. Nyerere was
aware that the electoral process could have little meaning
when only candidates of the single national party could be
nominated. Accordingly, he instituted a system, first at the
level of local elections and then nationally, by which candidates' names could be submitted to the local party executive
on petition of twenty-five voters. From the names submitted,
the local executive chose three, one of whom was to be
elected. Candidates were then given equal time to present
their platforms to the voters as individuals, but under the
overall umbrella of the national political party, the Tan-
ganyika African National Union. While candidates were not
expected to be in disagreement with the national policies of
the party, they were free to express individual points of
view, particularly on those issues affecting regional or local
conditions.

Experience thus far has proved the system to be reasonably effective in providing the voters with real alternatives
in selecting those who represent them. Given the relatively
limited spread of education in the rural areas, it is probable
that the electorate as a whole is neither competent to express,
nor interested in expressing, opinions on the broader issues
of national and international involvement of Tanzania in
the world community. It is content to leave the choice of
policy directions to the national party leadership in whom

[4] From *Black Africa: The Growing Pains of Independence,* pamphlet by
L. Gray Cowan, dean of the Graduate School of Public Affairs, State University of New York at Albany. (Headline Series No 210) Foreign Policy
Association. 345 E. 46th St. New York 10017. '72. p 18-19. Copyright © 1972 by
the Foreign Policy Association, Inc. Reprinted by permission.

there is general public confidence. But when it comes to local issues, such as the choice between building a school in the community or improving the water supply, the average villager has an informed opinion and can express it through a vote for that candidate who takes a position with which he agrees. If the chief objective of government is to demonstrate to the people as a whole the value of a system of popular choice, it may be more meaningful to lay emphasis on those issues upon which the voter does have some knowledge, rather than asking him to express an opinion on issues which are beyond the range of his interests.

The democratic tradition is, of course, far from alien to the traditional societies of black Africa; most ethnic groups had elements of democratic choice in the selection of leadership and in resolving issues affecting the group as a whole. The traditional African village meeting was an arena for the full and free expression of all shades of opinion, and the outcome of such discussion took the form of a consensus in which all adult members, having participated in the decision-making process, shared the results of a decision once taken, good or bad. At the end of a village meeting there remained no alienated minority which might form the basis for an ultimate split in the community. The difficulty has been to adapt this traditional system to the requirements of the modern technological world, which places limitations on both the time and the resources that can be used in evolving solutions to questions of development at the village level.

MILITARY INTERVENTION [5]

Independence was thought by many newly free peoples to be the beginning of the millennium. To be sure, there were some intimations of difficulties—but at least implied in the declarations of nationalist leaders was the belief that a country run like hell by the indigenous population was

[5] From *Politics of the Developing Nations*, by Fred R. von der Mehden, professor of political science, Rice University. 2d ed. Prentice-Hall. '69. p 100-3. Copyright © 1969 by Prentice-Hall, Inc., Englewood Cliffs, New Jersey. Reprinted by permission.

preferable to one run like heaven by a colonial administration. But the myth of freedom demanded that social, economic, and political progress quickly follow independence. And under the civilian politicians, this promise was not fulfilled: Pakistan, Ghana, and Sudan suffered from corruption, division, and maladministration; Burma foundered under twelve years of revolts, interparty strife, and administrative ineptitude; Indonesia never achieved the unity proclaimed in her national motto and faltered economically in spite of the numerous panaceas offered by Sukarno; Laos, South Vietnam, Nigeria, and the Congo were racked by internal warfare.

Under these conditions, the army began to reconsider the purely military role it had held during the colonial period: Burma, Pakistan, and Sudan came under army control in 1958; the government of Laos was taken over by the military during the next year; civilian government of the Congo Republic lasted only a few months; the military deposed and allegedly assassinated Ngo Dinh Diem in South Vietnam in 1963; then came a rash of coups in Africa as Nigeria, Dahomey, Sierra Leone, Ghana, Mali, and Algeria were among the new African states to suffer coups in the first decade of their independence.

The publicly announced reasons for these intrusions displayed a remarkable similarity. General Mirza, who with Ayub Khan led a successful coup in Pakistan in 1958, claimed:

I saved the country from a disaster which would have been bloody revolution. . . . It has so many dangerous compromises that Pakistan would disintegrate internally if the inherent sickness were not removed.

To do this, he proposed "to get twenty to thirty good clear chaps together to draw up a new constitution," which—at some future date—would be subject to popular referendum. General Abboud of Sudan promised:

In changing the prevailing state of affairs, we are not after personal gain, nor are we motivated by any hatred or malice toward anyone. Our aim is the stability, prosperity, and welfare of this country and its people.

The army in Burma reiterated these declarations but became somewhat more poetic when it compared its activities to those of Hercules in cleaning the Augean stables. However, these self-portrayals present an incomplete picture of the political and social milieux that instigated the armies' break with their apolitical traditions.

In most cases, these newly independent states have been racked by internal or external conflicts that have demanded continuous military alertness. Pakistan has been bedeviled by the problems attendant on partition, Kashmir, and the Afghan border. Burma has since 1947 faced revolts by the White Flag Communists, the Red Flag Communists, PVO [People's Volunteer Organization] forces, the Karens [and] the Shans [tribal groups] and the KMT [Kuomintang]. Indonesia has been plagued by insurrections in the outer islands as well as by conflicts with the Dutch over West Irian and the Malaysians over Borneo. The Laotian government has been the victim of a grim game of political musical chairs. And the Congo, Nigerian, and Vietnamese crises need no elaboration. As a rule the African states have not found this factor vital.

These conflicts are doubly significant in explaining the frustration and dissatisfaction of the military. First, the army—almost exclusively involved in military operations— was not tainted with the corruption and maladministration charges leveled at the civilian government; thus it appeared to be the reasonable alternative to the faltering politicians. Second, some members of the military undeniably felt that their operations in the field had been impeded by the ineptitude and bickering of the civilians. It was believed that efficient military control could more quickly solve other conflicts in which the army was involved. In Pakistan and Korea, this presumption proved to be correct.

Although other factors must be emphasized, that which usually triggered army intervention was the deterioration

of the civilian governments to the point at which civil war
—or at least bloodshed—threatened. In Burma, the split in
the AFPFL [Anti-Fascist Peoples' Freedom League], which
had ruled the country since independence, had produced a
real danger of civil war when General Ne Win stepped in.
In Indonesia, Nasution gained considerable stature after the
series of revolts in the outer islands during 1958. Among the
reasons given by Mobutu for his gamble for power in the
Congo [now Zaïre] was the fear of further bloodshed.

Yet these factors do not sufficiently explain why the army
was the chief alternative to the faltering politicians. Several
facets in the social and political life of these nations appear
responsible for this choice. First, the educated group from
which political leadership is drawn is pitifully small and
therefore provides only a small reserve of new leaders. Second, the economic life of the nation is usually in the hands
of nonindigenous elements; in fact, in many of the states,
the people view commerce as a profession with disdain. However, the party bureaucracy has tended to keep aspiring
young people from winning positions in the civilian government, making the army the only road to status, power, and
the achievement of personal and national social and economic gain. And when the civilian politicians prove unable
to cope with the problems of independence, the army takes
over.

The background of the military leadership is another
reason why the army is the chief alternative. The military
elite of the states under consideration can be divided into
two groups: those who participated in the nationalist movements and were politically oriented (as in Burma, the
Congo, Vietnam, and Indonesia); and those who were primarily apolitical professional soldiers (as in Pakistan, Sudan, Nigeria, Ghana, and the former French black African
states). In the first instance, the army could present itself as
the "true" and "unsullied" heir of independence—the one
sector of the nationalist movement unblemished by corruption and maladministration. The second group could por-

tray itself as the apolitical and unselfish protector of the national interest, pointing to its former military record as confirmation.

In the older Afro-Asian states (Egypt, Iraq, Iran, Jordan, Thailand, and Turkey), where the military has intervened in political life, similar factors are found. In the Middle East, the Arab-Israeli dispute led to bitterness and frustration with the corrupt and inept civilian governments of the Arab nations. . . . In all these states the military class developed as part of the small, educated elite.

THE ARMY IN AFRICA [6]

On independence day the African armies were essentially nonpolitical and nonconspiratorial. Their European and African officers fully expected to continue serving the new regime as they had the old. The African officers accepted the Western doctrines of civilian supremacy and a nonpolitical army, learned by example of the colonial powers and by precept at Sandhurst and St. Cyr [the British and French military academies].

Virtually all African armies continued to be heavily dependent upon European officers and advisers and on material support provided by the former metropolitan power. Even in such countries as Ghana and Nigeria, where the Africanization of the officer ranks was most advanced, European officers continued to predominate in top command and training positions during the first several years of independence. All officers and most noncommissioned officers in the Congo were Belgian on independence day. As late as the end of 1968 all the top command positions in Zambia's army were held by British officers; the highest Zambian officer was a major. Though the top positions in the armies of Kenya and Tanzania had been Africanized by 1968, both govern-

[6] From *Spear and Scepter: Army, Police, and Politics in Tropical Africa,* by Ernest W. Lefever, senior fellow, Brookings Foreign Policy Studies Program. Brookings. '70. p 18-22. Copyright © 1970 The Brookings Institution, Washington, D.C. Reprinted by permission.

ments employed high-level British officers as military advisers. Tanzania also employed Canadian officers.

During and following the transition to statehood in most
African countries the army was the strongest symbol of continuity between the old and the new orders. When the frail
and inexperienced regimes could not withstand the centrifugal forces unleashed by the withdrawal of externally imposed restraints, the military in a dozen states moved in to
fill the vacuum. The circumstances varied widely, but in
those where military intervention appeared justified to save
the state from disintegration, as in the Congo, or from dictatorship, as in Ghana, the officers were obviously uncomfortable in their unexpected role. Even in the islands of
relative political stability, such as the Ivory Coast and Kenya,
the army came to realize that simply by performing its classic
function it was in fact acting politically by siding with the
regime against its active or latent opponents.

Until recently, it had "occurred to few students . . . that
the military might become the critical group in shaping the
course of nation building"; scholars had assumed "the future of newly emergent states would be determined largely
by the activities of their westernized intellectuals, their so-
cialistically inclined bureaucrats, their nationalist ruling
parties, and possibly their menacing Communist parties."
(Lucian Pye. "Armies in the Process of Political Modernization." In *The Role of the Military in Underdeveloped
Countries*; ed. by J. J. Johnson. Princeton University Press.
1962. p 69.) In retrospect, the increasing political significance of the army and the police should have been more fully
anticipated. Military intervention should have come as no
surprise. With the grim backdrop of bloody turbulence in
many places in Asia and Latin America, why should the
less plausible states of Africa have been immune from conflict, coups, and chaos? In Africa, more than in any other
region, the army is a "heavy institution" in a light society
with a weak government. In such a "porous civilian-political
order the military have a capacity to act with authority and

force. As the army modernizes, a dangerous 'competence gap' grows between it and the rest of the community. The influx of technical training and ideas from industrialized countries underlines this point and widens the gap." (Fred Greene. In *Africa Report*. Feb. 1966.) As long as the central political symbols and institutions are weak and national cohesiveness is elusive—a condition that may persist for generations in most African countries—the politics of force will frequently supersede the politics of persuasion.

Army, Police, and Politics

The government of an independent territorial state must, by definition, have reliable instruments of coercion at its disposal to protect its people against internal and external dangers. No state can long endure unless it has an army or police force or their equivalents, or unless it is sustained by propitious equilibrium of internal and external forces. The scepter, a symbol of sovereign political authority, must be upheld by the men who wield the spear. This does not mean that governments are maintained on the points of spears, but that governments, sustained by the passive or active consent of their people, also must enjoy a monopoly of the legitimate use of violence within their territory. In any state—old or new, past or present—the military establishment by its very existence cannot avoid having a significant impact on political affairs, even when it refrains from acting.

In view of these classic political postulates, confirmed in everyday events, the scholarly neglect of the military (and police) in new states must be attributed to the modern movement away from classic political theory, an academic prejudice against the military as an institution, and a preoccupation with the more familiar noncoercive factors.

African armies tend to be the most detribalized, westernized, modernized, integrated, and cohesive institutions in their respective states. The army is usually the most disciplined agency in the state. It often enjoys a greater sense of national identity than other institutions. In technical skills, including the capacity to coerce and to communicate, the army is the most modernized agency in the country. It is the "best organized trade union," a potent pressure group competing for its slice of the meager state budget.

A more vivid symbol of sovereignty than the flag, the constitution, or the parliament, the army often evokes more popular sentiment than a political leader. The officer corps is an important and conspicuous component of the tiny ruling elite. In trim and colorful uniforms the army marches in independence day celebrations and its top brass stand with the head of state and prime minister on the reviewing platform. The political leaders understand only too well their dependence on the loyalty and effectiveness of the army in upholding their authority and in putting down any major challenge to the regime.

The military behavior of Africa's new states has been significantly affected by two factors that are commonly overlooked or underemphasized. One is the progressive, occasionally rapid, Africanization of the officer corps that has sometimes brought with it an erosion of professional skill and discipline. In some places it has led to a diminution of loyalty to the regime, a development that can be seen as positive or negative, depending upon one's view of the legitimacy and competence of the government in question. Some politicians, particularly in East Africa, have deliberately slowed the pace of Africanization, not only to maintain professional standards, but to assure military loyalty through the continued employment of British officers in command posts or as advisers.

The other phenomenon is temporary regression to earlier forms of tribal warfare. In the Congo, Nigeria, the Sudan, and elsewhere, Western rules of war—respect for civilians, fair treatment for prisoners, etc.—have given way to atavistic and brutal behavior that shows no mercy for civilians or prisoners and is more intent on ravishing the countryside for booty than achieving military objectives. This deterioration of discipline, usually associated with the breakdown of civil order, has occurred in part because of the absence of European or African officers trained in a tradition of civility. In the Western democratic world the chief function of the military is to deter and prevent war, while in the tribal tradition—particularly of the more aggressive tribes—the vocation of the warrior is to make war, to "wash his spear" in blood as it is sometimes put. The extent of this spear washing for revenge or for booty is determined in part by the remoteness of the area of combat from central civilian and military control, the intensity of the tribal hostility involved, and the professional quality of the government's junior officers and noncommissioned officers. In view of the deeply embedded warrior tradition that contemporary African armies must both build upon and restrain, it is fortunate that there have been no large interstate wars in Africa since independence.

THE MILITARY COUP: EFFORTLESS, INFECTIOUS [7]

By the time the coup d'état reached Africa, men of more blasé societies—whose own nation states had evolved through revolution and civil war, but in an earlier era—were already adapted. The Sierra Leone coup, said a United States Embassy official in Freetown, was just a Mickey Mouse show. African countries, said the skeptics, were like television stars: in the news with a coup today, forgotten tomorrow, or confused with each other in a succeeding coup.

It has proved infectious, this seizure of government by armed men, and so effortless. Get the keys of the armory; turn out the barracks; take the radio station, the post office and the airport; arrest the person of the president, and you arrest the state. In the Congo [Zaïre], where the new state disintegrated so disastrously so soon after independence, Colonel Mobutu, army chief-of-staff, "clarified" the situation by taking the capital with two hundred men. At the time it

[7] From *Power in Africa*, by Ruth First, South African exile who lives in London and travels extensively through Africa. Penguin African Library. Baltimore, Md. '72. p 4-6. Copyright © 1970 by Ruth First. Reprinted by permission of Pantheon Books/a Division of Random House, Inc.

was a larger force than any other single person controlled in Leopoldville. In Dahomey, General Soglo, who had come to power by a coup d'état, was overthrown by sixty paratroopers in December 1967. In Ghana 500 troops, from an army of 10,000 toppled supposedly one of the most formidable systems of political mobilization on the continent. In the Sudan two bridges over the Nile command Khartoum; and the unit that gets its guns into position first, commands the capital. In Dahomey a Minister of Foreign Affairs was heard to boast about one of that country's three coups d'état, that not a shot had been fired, not even a blank; not a teargas grenade had been thrown; and not a single arrest had been made. Dahomey's army men staged three coups in five years and thus far hold the record for Africa.

It seems to be done with little more than a few jerks of the trigger-finger; and there are, often, no casualties; Nigeria and Ghana were exceptions. Sierra Leone had fewer than half a hundred officers in her army by 1968. The coup that toppled the military government, itself brought to office by a coup d'état a year earlier, was organized by privates and by noncommissioned officers. The army consisted of one battalion. A barracks on a lovely flowered hillside in the capital was the single power center. The billiards room in the officers' mess was the scene of a brief tussle for control. The following morning, the debris was slight; some broken Coca-Cola bottles and cues lying awry on the green baize, and, in a ditch not far from the barracks, a car belonging to an officer who had tried to escape. After this coup, the entire army was in the control of two officers recalled from abroad —the rest was confined to the Pademba Road police station —and the police force was in the hands of two officers brought back from retirement. In Ghana Colonel Afrifa, or, as he came to be called after promotion, the Young Brigadier, was criticized for the detail he included in his chronicle of the Ghana coup. All that a conspirator had to do was read the relevant chapter, it was said. Lieutenant Arthur did, in fact, stage an abortive countercoup a year later, following much the same pattern as Afrifa had outlined. There had not yet been an instance of a lieutenant staging a successful coup in Africa, said Arthur. He aimed to be the first to do so. For the formation of the new military junta, he had counted out all colonels and above.

The facility of coup logistics and the audacity and arrogance of the coup makers are equaled by the inanity of their aims, at least as many choose to state them. At its face value, the army ethos embodies a general allergy to politicians; a search for unity and uprightness; and service to the nation. Nigeria's First Republic collapsed, said General Gowon, because it lacked high moral standards. Nzeogwu, the young major who made that particular coup, talked in more fevered but comparable terms of a strong, united and prosperous Nigeria, free from corruption and internal strife. In the Central African Republic, Colonel Jean Bedel Bokassa's Revolutionary Council announced a campaign to clean up morals, that would forbid drum-playing and lying about in the sun except on Saturdays and holidays. Colonel Lamizana of Upper Volta said, "The people asked us to assume responsibility. The army accepts." It is the simple soldier's view of politics, a search for a puritan ethic and a restoration of democracy unsullied by corrupt politicians. It is as though, in the army books and regulations by which the soldiers were drilled, there is an entry: *Coups, justification for*; and beside it, the felicitous phrases that the coup makers repeat by rote.

The coup is becoming conventional wisdom not only among Africa's army men, but among her young intellectuals. In the exile cafés of Paris and the bed-sitters of London, and on the university campuses of the United States, young aspirants for power, or social change, consider the making or unmaking of African governments in terms of their contacts within the army. Power changes hands so easily at the top, and the political infrastructure is so rapidly rendered tractable. Government shifts in a single night from State House to barracks. There are fresh names, ranks and titles to be learned. The photographers ready their cameras for the new official pictures: uniforms instead of double-breasted suits; the open army look instead of the politician's knowing glance. In place of laws lengthily disputed in debating chambers, come swift decrees in civil service jargon. There is more punctuality, less pomp, total pragmatism. "Efficiency" becomes the outstanding political principle. Political argument, once exuberantly fatuous in the mouths of career politicians, is stilled. In the political vacuum where the soldiers rule, the role and purpose of armed men go unquestioned. At the outset, it is enough for them to announce that they rule for the nation. Power lies in the hands of those who control the means of violence. It lies in the barrel of a gun, fired or silent.

A REVOLUTIONARY LEADER: UGANDA'S AMIN [8]

President [Idi] Amin, who seized power in a coup in January, 1971, has risen from obscurity to world notoriety in recent months [the fall of 1972]. As he has done so he has become more unpredictable. . . .

He has announced one "invasion" threat after another, accusing Britain, Israel, India and "NATO powers" in statements. He has said that Tanzanian troops were embarked on the waters of Lake Victoria and Indian troops on "destroyers in the Indian Ocean."

At the same time, he assures Ugandans not to worry because the twelve-thousand-man army can handle any threat.

President Amin, a burly Muslim from northwest Uganda, was an enlisted man in the King's African Rifles during British colonial days. He rose from sergeant major to colonel in five years as independence approached and came. Ironically, he was leap-frogged to army commander by Milton Obote, the civilian president he later overthrew.

[8] From "The Situation in Idi Amin's Uganda: Unpredictability Is the Order of the Day," by Charles Mohr, staff correspondent. New York *Times*. p 4. O. 12, '72. © 1972 by The New York Times Company. Reprinted by permission.

President Amin remains the quintessential African sergeant. In the army crisis growing out of the coup, most enlisted men seemed to favor him. Most field-grade officers seemed to disappear after he came to power.

Part of President Amin's behavior may possibly be explained by lack of sophistication.

At a simple level, diplomats report that he merely turned up at short notice in two of the state visits he made to foreign countries last year without an invitation—apparently not realizing one was required.

At a more complex level, President Amin . . . [in 1971] threatened to discharge or otherwise discipline civil servants if they were caught saying Uganda was bankrupt.

President Amin has shown little appreciation of economic problems or financial restraint and his threat was an indication that it was increasingly pointless for civil servants to try to exercise restraint.

Lack of experience and sophistication, however, cannot explain fully President Amin's actions and rhetoric.

His style could be called government—or politics—by escapism.

By ordering the crash construction of eight military airfields, military barracks and other projects, President Amin ran up a short-term debt to Israeli contractors of close to $18 million, which could not be paid.

This was probably not the only reason, but he shortly thereafter expelled all Israelis and became a loud critic of Zionism, going so far . . . as to praise Hitler's extermination of the Jews. [See following article for further information.]

The hasty and apparently unplanned mass expulsion of Asian business and professional men from Uganda may prove to be his most costly decision, although it had an immediate appeal to many black Ugandans.

What prompted the decision is not clear, unless one takes at face value President Amin's own assertion that God spoke to him in a dream. If, however, it was meant to divert attention from a growing financial squeeze, it can do so only temporarily because the Asian exodus will mean some, and possibly much, stagnation, in commerce and drastically reduce tax revenues in coming months.

As pressing as is the problem of economic decline, it may be less vital than that of discipline in President Amin's army. Leading Ugandans, including the vice chancellor of the university, some professors, ex-civil-servants and others have continued to vanish in the last month. The regime says that they "decided to disappear."

Although many hundreds and, more probably, thousands of Ugandans have "disappeared" since 1971, only a handful of cases have ever been solved and President Amin seems unwilling or unable to crack down on his army.

But, although the disappearances here have scarcely been dealt with, President Amin dramatically and angrily dismissed one army officer . . . [in 1972] for stealing a civilian's wife.

DESERT UPSTART: LIBYA'S KADDAFI [9]

Muammar Kaddafi [Moamar al-Gaddafi] is one of the worst-equipped of the world's rulers to assume power over the destiny of a nation. The son of a Bedouin barley farmer, he was educated in Islamic schools and Libya's Royal Military Academy, had no experience in economics or administration—and discovered what he knew of politics from listening to the radio speeches of his idol, the late President Nasser of Egypt. "When we first found out who was leading the revolution," a Tripoli businessman who now supports Kaddafi told me, "we shuddered."

Return to Islamic Roots

As a devout Moslem, Kaddafi made it one of his first acts upon seizing power [in 1969] to return Libya to its Islamic roots. Although his country was a major exporter of wine, he forbade the sale and production of alcohol. Of-

[9] From "Libya: The Desert Upstart," by Loren Jenkins, staff correspondent. *Newsweek.* 80:36+. S. 11, '72. Copyright © Newsweek, Inc. 1972, reprinted by permission.

fended by the honky-tonk atmosphere in Tripoli, he per-
sonally cruised the city in a gray Volkswagen, seeking out
sin and moral transgressions and, in the process, closing
down two of the city's belly-dance nightclubs. And after he
noticed that the Roman Catholic cathedral in the center of
the city was taller than any mosque, he ordered it converted
to the Gamal Abdel Nasser Mosque and had its crosses replaced with the crescent and stars of Islam. He also expelled
the fifteen thousand Italians who provided most of his country's skilled labor and in the process transformed a relatively
gay, Italian-flavored port into one of the drabbest cities on
the Mediterranean.

Kaddafi has also established himself as something of an
enfant terrible of world politics. He forced both Britain and
the United States to give up their air bases in Libya and
squeezed new arrangements out of Western oil interests that
have since doubled his country's income. But if the West has
taken some hard knocks from the desert upstart, the Soviet
Union has fared even worse. Kaddafi has denounced all
treaties by Arab governments with the Soviets, rejoiced when
a Communist coup failed in the Sudan last year and openly
criticized Egyptian President Anwar Sadat for permitting a
Soviet military presence in his country. Kaddafi also promised Sadat more economic support if he would throw the
Russians out, which the Egyptian President did. . . .

Revolutionary Causes

In addition, Kaddafi has pledged to use his country's
$2.4 billion annual oil income to help bankroll such revo-
lutionary causes as the Black Panthers in the United States,
the Irish Republican Army, and Moslem rebels in the Philippines. He has also used Libya's affluence to talk a reluctant
Sadat into starting talks that are supposed to result in a
merger of the two countries.

But his dearest enterprise is the Arab confrontation with
Israel, and for that undertaking he has donated large
amounts of money to the Palestinian commandos and sent

three hundred Libyans to fight with them. Kaddafi has also given $26 million to Uganda, in exchange for which the eccentric leader of that East African country, President Idi Amin, has expelled Israeli technicians and adopted a pro-Arab policy.

For Kaddafi, the confrontation with Israel is a *jihad,* a holy war [said one diplomat in Tripoli]. When it is won, he wants to expel all who have settled in Palestine since 1948, while those Jews and Christians that were there before are to be allowed to live on as protected minorities under an Arab regime. The thing about Kaddafi is that he really thinks that this scheme is feasible.

In his three years in power, Kaddafi has not always had his way in the Revolutionary Command Council, and one of these days it is possible that his fellow revolutionaries will find it possible to dispense with his charismatic leadership. But for the time being, despite all his posturing and erratic decision making, he is still going strong. The open secret of his success is the oil money. With it, he has been able to buy himself into a position of leadership in the Arab world and embark on a development program at home that has led to an economic resurgence.

Signs of that resurgence are everywhere in Tripoli. To be sure, one still sees slums built of tin cans and orange crates that put the notorious Palestine refugee camps to shame. But just down the road there are massive housing projects being rushed to completion. The port itself bustles with activity as dockers unload everything from heavy machinery to Italian sewing machines and Japanese transistor radios. New European cars career through the streets, and Libya already boasts one of the largest car ownerships per capita in the world. "For all his rhetoric," a Western economist told me, "Kaddafi is trying to give his people a better life."

But it is not just money and economic progress that explain Kaddafi's emergence among the Arab masses as something akin to Nasser's successor. "Always a race in search of a messianic leader on a white charger," says one Middle East analyst, "the Arabs admire Kaddafi for his independence, sincerity and unflagging efforts to advance their cause."

KIM OF NORTH KOREA: THE LAST STALINIST [10]

There are . . . aspects and experiences which seem to set North Korea apart in space, time and political behavior. Now and then one detects a touch of the Soviet Union or China—but it is distinctly a Russia or China of another day.

It is a land of dated slogans. A busy intersection is ablaze at night with the lights of a huge sign reading, "Let Us Defend With Our Lives the Central Committee of the Workers Party, Headed by Comrade Kim Il Sung." Another sign, with a crossed hammer and rifle, says, "Economic Construction and National Defense." At the circus, an acrobat spinning on a rotating wheel unfurls a banner reading, "Long Live the *Juche* [self-reliance, independence] Idea of Our Great Leader, Comrade Kim Il Sung!" At the Children's Palace, a performance concludes, à la Peking at the height of the Cultural Revolution, with the image of a radiant sun with the North Korean Premier's face superimposed on it.

It is a land of obedience, discipline and a kind of respect for authority that will not be found elsewhere in the Communist world. We travel about in a large, old, black Soviet-made limousine with white curtains on the windows. We can look out, but the passerby cannot clearly see us. As we drive down the highway, the peasants and school children give the car a waist-deep bow. After all, a black car represents Authority. . . .

The Works of Kim

Every town, village, factory, school and army barrack in North Korea has an elaborate "study hall," where young and old alike, men and women, gather to discuss, for the *nth* time, the "guidance offered by the beloved and respected leader." My official companion tells me a well-arranged day

[10] From "The Cult of Kim," by Mark Gayn, columnist for *The Toronto Star*. New York *Times Magazine*. p 16+. O. 1, '72. © 1972 by The New York Times Company. Reprinted by permission.

should consist of eight hours of sleep, eight of work, and eight of studying Kim's works. In fact, everyone is required to devote two hours to Kim-study daily, and four hours on Saturday. In a primary school, I find children chanting a chapter from a 480-page book, the first volume of *Let's Study the Great Revolutionary Idea of Marshal Kim Il Sung*. They are to have memorized it by the year's end. There are five volumes, and the students are required to commit them all to memory. (I am not told if this is ever attained.) The backbone on which the flesh of Korean Marxism hangs is Kim's official biography, depicted in word and painting in every "study hall" and school. . . .

Reality vs. Fiction

Experts who have watched Kim for decades find his official biography, to put it mildly, inexact. After the Japanese seized Manchuria in September 1931, these experts say, the Soviet Union decided, as a measure of self-protection, to form Korean and Chinese guerrilla units to harass the Japanese Kwantung Army. There were a number of these small bands, and one of them—a hundred men or fewer—was headed by Kim. The units made hit-and-run raids and now and then crossed the Soviet border for R and R. Rested, recuperated and, one might add, reequipped, they soon returned to the Manchuria mountains.

Sometime after the Soviet-Japanese pocket war in the fall of 1939, the two sides finally reached an accommodation. The guerrilla bands were withdrawn from Manchuria. Presented with the problem of feeding, housing and paying the Koreans, the Soviet Government solved it on the basis of unit size. Because Kim's unit was roughly company-size, he was given the rank and pay of a captain in the Soviet Army. His was neither the largest nor the best-known of the guerrilla units. He remained in the Soviet Far East until after the end of the war. Kim, in the words of a Communist historian, "was brought to Wongsan, as I remember, in October 1945, in a supply column of the Red Army." The Japanese

Army had surrendered almost two months earlier, to the Soviet command. And Korean Communist groups which remained underground during the Japanese occupation surfaced in Pyongyang before Kim appeared.

The postwar Communist leaders came from the alleyways of Pyongyang, from Mao Tse-tung's guerrilla areas in China and from Moscow. Many were more able than Kim. But in casting about for the head of Communist Korea, Stalin chose Kim.

> You must understand Stalin [says a Communist specialist]. He was a supremely suspicious man, who saw spies under his breakfast table. To him, all the Communists who remained in the underground in Japanese-held Korea were potential spies. . . . Kim had spent five or six years in the Soviet Union, and his biography was transparent. He was a limited man, a guerrilla rather than an ideologue, a man of whose loyalty Stalin had no doubt. Thus, the choice fell on Kim. . . .

. . . Kim has been in full control ever since—the last Stalinist still in power. [He weathered two crises when his authority was challenged: the Korean war and Nikita Khrushchev's denunciation of Stalin in 1956.] But he is no longer the man on whose loyalty Stalin thought he could always count. It is impossible to know what has changed Kim. Perhaps it was the general current of independence that has been coursing through the smaller Communist states since Khrushchev's speech in 1956. Perhaps it was the sight of the squabble between Moscow and Peking, and the impact it has had on the Communist movement. Or, it may have been Moscow's failure to provide as much economic aid as the North Koreans wanted. At any rate Kim has been pursuing an increasingly independent line. In effect, he has become in Asia what Rumania's Nicolae Ceausescu has been in East Europe. In the process of gaining his independence, Kim has also mastered the ancient but still intricate art of playing his powerful patrons off against each other. . . .

Twenty-seven years after he was installed in Pyongyang, the last surviving Stalinist (Albania's Enver Hoxha is a

Maoist) has discovered that a Stalinist foreign policy can no longer be effective. He is trying to adapt himself and his policies to the new realities. But he must also persuade the outside world that he is a moderate statesman seeking peace. He must convince the people in the south that he has given up his earlier ideas and methods of reuniting the land. He must be a liberal abroad without liberalizing the Stalinist regime at home. And, sooner or later, he must somehow come to terms with the United States and Japan without abandoning his essential anti-American and anti-Japanese propaganda.

None of this is easy. But, then, which Communist leader in Asia is finding life easy in this season of flux, *détente*— and Marxist heresy?

INDIA: "ORDEAL OF NATIONHOOD" [11]

The next decade may carry for India bigger dangers and uncertainties than those it has encountered in the past. Some of the major challenges appear to be ahead, not behind. In fact, so far India has led what a combination of circumstances has made a rather sheltered, unreal life. Nehru's personality gave India an exaggerated, almost artificial sense of national unity. Under his leadership, the Centre [federal government] exercised authority that was warranted neither by the Constitution nor by Indian temperament. His presence sustained political institutions, administrative practices and social attitudes that were foreign to the land. Besides Nehru's dominance, other advantages that India enjoyed in the early years of independence have been dissipated by now. The euphoric self-confidence created by the success of the freedom movement is gone; so is the stimulation that the economy received from World War II and the accumulation of enormous sterling resources. The administrative structure that it had inherited from the British is still there, but the

[11] From *The Ordeal of Nationhood: A Social Study of India Since Independence, 1947-1970,* by Krishan Bhatia, foreign correspondent of the Hindustan *Times.* Atheneum. New York. '71. p 363-9. Copyright © 1971 by Krishan Bhatia. Reprinted by permission of Atheneum Publishers.

once-streamlined instrument of power has grown into a vast, amorphous bureaucracy that has obstinately retained some of the negative attitudes cultivated during the days of the Raj but has acquired few positive virtues suited to the needs of the new society.

It was not until well after Nehru's death that India slowly started the process of coming to terms with its true self, its politics began to find its real level, and its institutions and practices were molded to match the country's special character. It will be several years before the change is completed —an interim during which the capacity of India's leadership, the strength of its administration and economy and its instinct for survival will be subjected to severe strains. It may be apparent only toward the end of the seventies whether India will succumb to regional and parochial pulls or continue to live as a united nation and, if the latter is the case, whether it will grow into a modern-minded, prosperous nation.

The country's political prospects present what is probably the least depressing aspect of the picture. After [Lal Bahadur] Shastri's sudden death in the beginning of 1966, India appeared to be without a nationally accepted leader. Mrs. Gandhi, who succeeded him as prime minister, was unsure of herself and, though respected as Nehru's daughter, was not considered a leader in her own right. Others behind her could at best command local and regional followings. Since her confrontation with the right-wing "syndicate" in her party, however, Mrs. Gandhi has appeared to be growing into a leader of national stature. . . .

Outside the legislature, the task before Mrs. Gandhi or any other leader who might come to the top is less overwhelming than it may seem. Indian masses do not make exacting demands on their leaders. Once a leader's *bona fides* . . . [is] established, Indians give him their affection and trust in generous measures, and their capacity to overlook the leader's mistakes or shortcomings is considerable. In the hands of a strong leader whose integrity is not doubted,

such a people can be strongly directed to positive action.
Some of the causes for divisiveness, moreover, appear to be
subsiding.

The Bureaucracy

Unless drastic remedial action is taken soon, India's administration may collapse under its own weight. The central
and state governments, state-controlled corporations and
various local administrations now employ nearly eleven
million officials—several times the size of the bureaucracy
at the time of independence. Government involvement in
the lives of the people has increased markedly since the time
of the British, and it was inevitable that the number of its
functionaries should grow. But the increase has been far out
of proportion to the increase in their responsibilities—and
certainly to their productivity.

Administrative experts have often bemoaned the Indian
bureaucracy's tendency to obstruct rather than facilitate the
process of governance. Mrs. Gandhi herself has spoken with
unconcealed exasperation about being hamstrung by the
officials around her and her helplessness to prod them into
purposeful action. Few administrations are so paper-bound
as India's. Most civil servants have a Brahminical penchant
for theorizing and a marked aversion to action. Under the
British, the average official was expected to quote rules and
regulations and then await direction from the top. He still
retains that colonial attitude of mind and will not make a
decision if he can maneuver someone above him into giving
him an order. As under the British, he tends to play it safe
and devotes time and energy to protecting himself against
any possible criticism rather than to making a sensible decision quickly. That members of Parliament often ask searching questions about official actions and legislative bodies
sometimes probe them with almost judicial thoroughness
has only added to his nervousness and desire to shield himself completely before taking even a small step. The result

is a constant shuffling of official files from table to table, interminable interdepartmental conferences in an unabashed bid to diffuse responsibility, and over-all delays of a kind that a country with so much to accomplish cannot afford.

While refusing to shed some of its outdated methods and habits, the bureaucracy has shown an enormous appetite for personal power and, particularly at lower levels, a distressing capacity for graft and corruption. In the name of socialism, the civil service has usurped a sizable area of national activity as its exclusive preserve and then proceeded to administer it indifferently and unenthusiastically. . . .

Yet, notwithstanding its mistakes and inadequacies, one must not judge India with undue harshness. What it has set itself to accomplish is a truly enormous task. It is trying to bring about a virtual revolution without the kind of convulsive upheaval usual in an underdeveloped society seeking to become a modern nation almost overnight. It is hoping to achieve in two or three decades what others lingered over for centuries, and it intends to do so without bloodshed or impairment of personal liberties. In Britain, devolution of political power started with the signing of the Magna Carta in the thirteenth century; the process was completed only at the beginning of the twentieth century with the rise of the Labour Party. In India, power has passed in twenty years from princes and the Western-educated urban elite to the lower middle classes—and now seems within reach of the factory worker and the peasant. The caste system and other social structures that had remained unchanged for several thousand years have developed serious cracks since independence. That India should be manufacturing its own supersonic fighter aircraft while the bullock cart, the traditional symbol of its backwardness, is nowhere near obsolescence yet characterizes the size of the task before India as well as the measure of success it has so far achieved.

MARTIAL LAW IN THE PHILIPPINES [12]

There once were two presidents. The first governed his country for seven years, during which time crime and corruption, perhaps always endemic in the society, became epidemic. Warlords, some of them the president's own vassals, ruled personal and political fiefdoms with private armies. The grand canyon separating rich and poor grew wider, the "green revolution" in the countryside faltered. Land-reform laws lay largely unimplemented. Unemployment rose. The political process became increasingly irrelevant to the real needs of the people, and the people became increasingly alienated from the political process. Communism gained converts, or at least listeners, particularly among the young. The president himself dealt in the traditional politics of patronage and pork barrel and, in the process, became a millionaire many times over.

The second president spoke out against that shocking state of affairs. He proclaimed a "new society" in which the corruptions and machinations of old-style politics would be ended, crime and graft would be combated, a sense of discipline and of purpose would be instilled in the people, social reforms would be implemented and the economy would prosper.

When Two Equals One

The problem, or at least the paradox, of all this is that the two presidents are one: Ferdinand E. Marcos of the Philippines, who, two weeks ago, proclaimed martial law over what has probably been the world's most anarchic neodemocracy.

Few people here, Filipinos or foreigners, deny that this country is in urgent need of some discipline (or self-discipline) and of many reforms—indeed, of some sort of new (or renewed) society.

[12] From "The New Manila: Marcos' Martial Law Is Not Very Martial—But Is It Justified?" by Peter R. Kann, staff reporter. *Wall Street Journal.* p 1+. O. 11, '72. Reprinted with permission of *The Wall Street Journal.*

But the manner in which President Marcos now is oper-
ating, his motivations, his justifications and his chances of
success—all these are much in question.

For better or worse, President Marcos has unilaterally
changed the rules by which the game of government has been
played ever since the Philippines was granted independence
by the United States in 1946. And, if there now is a new
opportunity for progress and reform and for the president
to emerge as a hero, there is at least some risk that ends
won't justify means and that the future could flow not in the
direction of reform but toward repression and revolution.

Unmartial Martial Law

Filipinos aren't a very martial people, and the martial
law the president declared two weeks ago, so far at least, has
been distinctly Filipino and decidedly unmartial. . . .

"No bloodshed, no tanks, no machine guns, no barbed
wire—we have the best martial law in the whole world," says
Memesio Yabut, a Marcos booster, who is mayor of a Manila
suburb. If the Roman Emperor Caligula once wished that
"the Roman people had but one neck" to wring, the most
that President Marcos seems to be wishing is that the Pilip-
pine people had but one wrist to slap.

And yet much more has been lost . . . in the last two
weeks than is lost when martial law is declared in most
third-world nations. The Philippines certainly wasn't a
model democracy, but neither is it a banana-republic kind
of country.

Philippine democracy was the product of an arranged
marriage between an oligarchic and exploitative feudal society and virginal American democratic institutions. The
offspring was a kind of satyr—half-goat and half-man—that
ran about rather happily, rather violently and more than
rather irresponsibly. But, if only because one parent was
democracy, the Philippines has been more of a democracy
than almost any other country in Asia.

It's still premature to sing funeral dirges for Philippine democracy. Technically at least, the proclamation of martial law was legal under the Philippine constitution. Congress is adjourned but hasn't been disbanded. The military is doing the bidding of the president, not ruling on its own. This isn't a nation of fear, though it is a nation in which critics now speak softly and guardedly and certainly don't want to be quoted. . . .

If the need for martial law or at least for some sort of change is widely accepted, the justification for its imposition is not. Under the constitution of the Philippines, martial law can be imposed in case of an imminent threat to overthrow the government. In his proclamation of martial law, the president mentioned what he called the threat from the Communist "New Peoples Army" (NPA) and its "unmitigated forays, raids, ambuscades, assaults, violence, murders, assassinations, acts of terror, deceits, coercions, threats, intimidations, treachery, machinations, arsons, plunders and depredations." . . .

There has been a "Communist threat" in the Philippines since before World War II—under various names and with varying levels of activity and support. But three days before martial law was declared, the National Security Council was told by the generals that the internal security situation was between normal and Internal Defense Condition 1, which means localized threats requiring some supplemental national police support to some local areas. That is a situation that has been going on for years. Even the government's statistics on the Communist threat don't really seem so alarming: 1,000 armed regulars, 10,000 part-time supporters and 100,000 sympathizers—this in a nation of 40 million people.

Little Talk of Communism

While the Communist threat was cited as the formal justification for martial law, President Marcos has since been talking very little about communism and a great deal about social reforms and his new society. In effect, he has offered one justification to satisfy the constitution and another to try to satisfy the people. . . .

Even some of the president's propagandists tend to suggest that the Marcos of martial law is a new Marcos, which implies that there was something wrong with the old. In a sense, they are saying that martial law amounts to the new Marcos pulling off a coup against the old Marcos. . . .

What Does the Future Hold?

What the future holds for the Philippines seems to depend partly on the motivations and abilities of the president, partly on how "sick" (as the president has called it) the society really is and partly on the degree of the people's expectations. Some observers believe Philippine society is fundamentally corrupted. If this is true, a year or several of martial law may have little effect. Others say the sickness is more a skin disease than a problem of the internal organs.

The people's expectations are almost impossible to measure. Perhaps, as one diplomat puts it, "rice and sugar and peace and order are more than most Filipinos have had for a long time, and it will be enough to satisfy them for a long time." This thinking, of course, assumes that martial law can really hold down prices and crime. Other observers, however, contend that the new society will raise expectations for jobs, land and general prosperity and that the president will be under pressure on these issues within a year. . . .

The sixty-thousand-man Philippine armed forces so far have been following the president's orders, with approval and with considerable restraint. But at least some danger exists that the army will gradually begin to abuse its new authority, particularly out in the provinces, and come to be resented by the people. The Philippine army, unlike most others in Asia, has traditionally stayed out of political affairs. But the Philippine army now is being forced into such affairs and could come to develop its own political interests and one day pose a threat, if not to President Marcos then to one of his successors.

Such dangers are highly speculative, but it does seem fair to say that the situation in the Philippines has changed rather significantly . . . and that, for better or worse, the country will never be quite the same again.

CORRUPTION, PLAGUE OF NEW NATIONS, IN INDONESIA [13]

Corruption . . . has now become so institutionalized in Indonesia that its eradication, if that were conceivable, might mean the critical dislocation of the whole shaky national structure. For corruption has established itself as a means of escape, survival, and achievement in difficult times, and in Indonesia the times seem always to be frighteningly difficult. Corruption has become the now conventional unconventional device for dealing with irresolvable problems. It is especially but not exclusively useful in coping with the government and its infinitely numerous regulations, as mistily codified and masterfully maladministered by an obtuse and all-pervasive bureaucracy.

For years and years the great majority of urban Indonesians have experienced greater impediment than assistance on the part of their government in the achievement of their most basic, routine, normal objectives, such, for instance, as the procurement of food, clothing, housing, and jobs. In the Sukarno era irrationality, irresponsibility, and incongruity were the norm; in the Suharto era predictability and continuity have not been as much as half established. To take the example the Indonesians themselves most commonly cite, at almost any level of employment today, from lowest to highest, one month's wages or salary will just barely sustain a family for about one week. Marketplace factors such as supply and demand, cost and price, collection and distribution, taxation and subsidy are so irreconcilable as to make

[13] From *A Primer of "Korupsi,"* by Willard A. Hanna, associate of the American Universities Field Staff. (Southeast Asia Series. v 19, no 8) '71. p 1-4, 6-7. Copyright © 1971 by American Universities Field Staff, Inc. Reprinted by permission of the publisher.

of prudence a folly and of frugality an extravagance. Official agencies for the most part are still incapable of efficiently performing even the minimal services which are necessary to maintain a regime in decent order. They are deeply bogged down in their own bureaucratic controls, many of which were originally designed to stifle rather than to encourage enterprise unless officials were corrupted to ignore them. . . .

The new Indonesian nation, like many, many others new and old, is undergoing a prolonged and agonizing crisis of values, and the easy catchall category for the most distressing symptoms is corruption. The Indonesian word—and a careful word count would probably show it more common by far in Indonesian speech and writing today than such words as "revolution," "liberation," and "relevancy" in the West —is *korupsi*. The fact that the word *korupsi* itself is a corruption of a Western word adopted into the Indonesian language, which has no exact equivalent, might suggest that the current concept and practice are somehow alien to the Indonesian character. Indonesians make out no such self-justifying case. But their sudden emergence as an independent people into the vastly troubled modern world has in fact created the special situation in which *korupsi* is a national fixation. For lack of the dissertation which some sober scholar should already have written from the abundant materials now at hand, it may be instructive to put together at least a tentative primer on *korupsi* and its sociological significance in contemporary Indonesia.

A, then, stands for the Abduction, rape, arrest for "false accusation," imprisonment, interrogation, intimidation, court trial, and eventual release of seventeen-year-old Sum Kuning, a market stall girl of Jogjakarta. Sum Kuning had the misfortune to attract the attention of four youths, three of them longhairs, the sons of families so prominent that the names could only be whispered. Her subsequent ordeal, as finally brought out in the press and in court, shocked the nation. An inquiring journalist, who was himself detained and interrogated, a courageous woman judge who rejected the trumped-up police evidence, the national Chief of Police himself, who ordered a complete reinvestigation—these three became national heroes. Sum Kuning was cleared and freed, but her abusers are still at large and most of those who sought to frame her have not as yet themselves been exposed. The hope, nevertheless, remains that justice may still be done, not only as regards the girl herself but as regards the millions of other Indonesians who have experienced rape and plunder in feudal, colonial, and republican times.

The Sum Kuning story could be slightly rescripted for dozens of other countries, but in Indonesia, it is a clear if limited moral victory of the *rakjat* (people) over the *pembesar-pempenting* (big and important). Hence it is a signal that *korupsi*—in the sense not just of the misuse of money but the abuse of prestige and power—may soon be subject to long overdue restraints.

B stands for Baby, specifically the "Miraculous Baby" of 1970, whose story is the comic antithesis to the tragedy of Sum Kuning. In early 1970 a pair of transparently shady characters from Atjeh, Teuku Sjarifuddin and his wife Tjut Zahara, electrified the Indonesian nation with the news that Tjut was already two years pregnant with a "miraculous baby" who refused to be born except in Mecca. Meanwhile, the "baby" could be heard while still within the womb devoutly chanting long passages from the Koran in perfect Arabic. Various personages of unimpeachable credentials testified to the truth of the account. The press and public followed the case with avid interest while certain cabinet ministers and generals, among them General Nasution, and other prominent personages received the expectant parents or paid calls upon them, audited the Koranic recitations, and more or less officially and publicity declared themselves convinced. There were also skeptics, however, and after six months of excitement—while the couple was being lionized and also no doubt generously subsidized, visitations being occasion for gifts—came the denouement. Madame was not pregnant. The bulge in her belly was merely a bundle of spare lingerie and towels in which was concealed a miniature tape recorder. Tjut was arrested and jailed for "disturbing the peace with false report." She escaped when a shy guard permitted her to bathe unspied upon in the river which flowed past her prison; she was rearrested and again jailed and will probably one day soon be permitted quietly to vanish into the obscurity whence she came.

The case of the "miraculous baby" involved a minor element of financial swindle and hence of routine corruption. It involved a major element of artful deception and willful self-delusion and hence some of the worst aspects of the intellectual *korupsi* of the Sukarno era. The followers of Sukarno and his once hallowed teachings passionately rejected rationality in preference for credulity, relied upon the miraculous rather than the scientific, and branded their critics counterrevolutionaries. But just as the case of the miracle child symbolizes the Indonesian's addiction to the theatrical, which, in Sukarno times, substituted for the tedious labors of nation making, so too, fortunately, it demonstrates his cheerful capacity for laughing afterwards at his own absurdities. Although any charlatan can still command a clientele of VIPs, into this sort of *korupsi* there may be built the element of eventual self-cure.

C is for Commission on Corruption and the Curious Consequent Collusion to Circumvent the Concealment of its Confidential Catalogue of Cases. In response to press, student, and public pressures, President Suharto on January 31, 1970, appointed a four-man commission of distinguished elder statesmen, one of them ex-Vice-President Hatta, to make special report whether corruption really was as serious a national problem as the industrious muckrakers claimed. In a series of letters to the president over the next six months the Commission confirmed the most alarmist conjectures and gave attention to the causes and consequences. It also fingered half a dozen especially notorious official and private entities for priority investigation by the attorney general's strangely inactive Corruption Eradication Team, which rarely concedes that behind allegations, convincing though they might appear to the lay mind, there is any discernible legal evidence. Further to prompt the attorney general, the Commission dealt in great detail with the anomalous and especially corrupt practices within certain specific agencies and industries.

The Commission made careful inquiry, for instance, into the timber industry. It found that valuable concessions are being handed out illegally to slick foreign operators and their get-rich-quick Indonesian partners whose starting capital is knowledgeability about permits and payoffs. Indonesia's invaluable timber reserves, the Commission further pointed out, are being felled with little concern either for conservation or the assessment and collection of government royalties. . . .

The Commission's classified report, of which there were only four copies, each in presumably secure safekeeping, might have moldered away in the files had not some very highly placed person or persons leaked it in full to the press. It was published seriatim in mid-July [1971] by a leading Djakarta daily, *Sinar Harapan*, which was variously congratulated and condemned for its scoop, which other editors intimated had also been offered to them. To a Western reader the Commission report seems a model of diffusion and confusion, of oblique statement and implied conclusion. It was no less a sensation and a revelation, constituting as it did a top level exhortation to the attorney general speedily to get on with urgent business and telling him not exactly with whom (this would have meant fingering too many generals) but just where to start. . . .

The economic, social, and political significance of *korupsi* should be neither over- nor underestimated. In terms of national revenue, it seems safe to estimate that a minimal 25 percent gets siphoned off into—and also of course through —the pockets of corrupt operators. This rough and ready 25 percent factor for *korupsi* is higher than the 20 percent which is commonly mentioned in Thailand, lower than the 30 percent which is widely assumed in the Philippines. How it compares with percentages in the Western world is for yet more sophisticated generations of computers to calculate. Despite certain noteworthy reforms since 1965, *korupsi* is still on the increase. It has come to be regarded as both normal and necessary.

The great debate, which has in fact been going on intermittently for years, has now established the fact that *korupsi* is no mere press and youth fixation but a national problem of truly critical proportions. *Korupsi,* people conclude, must be eradicated—but no one seriously thinks that it will be or even that it will soon be much reduced.

CORRUPTION IN GHANA [14]

In March 1970 Mr. Justice P. D. Anin was named by the Ghanaian Presidential Commission, acting on the advice of the prime minister, to head a five-man Commission of Enquiry into Bribery and Corruption. Not only was it authorized "to study the area, prevalence, and methods of bribery and corruption in Ghanaian society," but also to determine whether there were factors in the society which contributed to this. "As a people, do we frown upon and resist bribery and corruption or do we tend to regard them as natural and inevitable?" asked Anin at the first meeting of the Commission of Enquiry on 29 June 1970, adding: "Do we draw a line between the 'customary drink' under our traditional practices, and bribery and corruption of public officers and others holding positions of trust?" The answers to these questions, it was hoped, would lead to recommendations for the eradication of these social evils.

In many countries of the world, a commission of inquiry of this sort is rare. Publicizing accusations of corruption

[14] From "The Roots of Corruption—the Ghanaian Enquiry," by Herbert H. Werlin, assistant professor, Department of Government and Politics, University of Maryland, College Park. *Journal of Modern African Studies.* 10: 247-62. Jl. '72. Reprinted by permission of the publishers, Cambridge University Press.

would be seen as politically embarrassing and as discrediting the civil service in such a way as to decrease its effectiveness. For Ghanaians, however, the only thing surprising about the appointment of the Anin Commission was that it was considered necessary. Ghana, after all, has carried out and published far more studies of corruption than any other country of Africa during the postcolonial period. . . .

The extent of corruption existing in Ghana under Nkrumah is amply documented by the more than forty commissions or committees of inquiry that were carried out after his ouster. A kickback of from 5 to 10 percent was expected in return for government contracts. The CPP [Convention People's Party] garnered about 90 percent of its income in this way, amounting to over $5 million between 1958 and 1966, which Nkrumah freely used for his own purposes. . . .

The postcoup government, of course, recognized the usefulness of these commissions of inquiry in discrediting the Nkrumah regime. Despite this fact, scholars have attested to their fairness and carefulness. . . .

The Causes of Corruption

David Apter, among other Western scholars, attributes corruption in Ghana to the persistence of traditional values which conflict with the requirements for a secular way of life: "Nepotism, for example, is considered a grave offense in Western bureaucratic practice, yet in African practice providing jobs for the members of one's own family is socially compulsory." Many Ghanaians would agree with this analysis; the more successful a civil servant or politician becomes, the more he is expected to share his good fortune with his kinsmen. "The family-conscious Ghanaian is hence terribly loaded with a proliferation of duties and obligations owed to relatives known and unknown who may spring up and demand attention when one is busily performing his official duties."

It is not uncommon for a Ghanaian family to consist of more than five hundred, and even the most distant relative can expect assistance. The welfare of the clan, Professor W. E. Abraham points out, is more important than the welfare of the individual. Moreover, the emphasis in African culture is achievement through clan cooperation rather than through self-help. Therefore, neglecting one's family is the most terrible thing that one can do. Generosity, on the other hand, is the most appreciated human quality. When a politician has been generous, even at public expense, all his other faults are forgiven. At the same time, a Ghanaian derives satisfaction as well as prestige from having people dependent on him.

To avoid accusations of ingratitude, politicians and top civil servants must surround themselves with their fellow tribesmen as well as their more immediate relatives. "I could not have chosen my government without some regard to tribal origins," Nkrumah admits, "and even, within the party itself, there was at times a tendency to condemn or recommend some individual on the basis of his tribal or family origin." Likewise, the giving and receiving of gifts becomes unavoidable. It would be a most unfriendly gesture for a minister to refuse the $200 gift that he commonly receives from each village that he visits, regardless of the obligations that this might entail. While gift giving is not necessarily seen as corruptive, it certainly leads to an expectation of reciprocation. What complicates this situation is the difficulty Ghanaians have in adjusting to the impersonal, disinterested, legalistic character of obligations required for the successful functioning of the modern bureaucracy. . . .

The need to grant favors to relatives and friends, one informant emphasized, is not so much a concern for custom as it is a concern for their unemployment and poverty. Where most of the relatives have jobs or reasonable incomes, as among the American or British bourgeoisie, they do not have to exert so much pressure for favorable treatment on those in high political positions. The keen competition for jobs is seen as one of the most important factors giving impetus to tribalism. It also meant that some Ghanaians were willing to sacrifice whatever integrity they had for the sake of employment. "This is because in a developing nation the government is the largest employer," notes J. K. Anoyke [in *The Ghanaian Times,* Feb. 13, 1970], "and this being the case, the government attracts all sorts of people, who only want their stomachs filled."

Poverty impels men not only to tolerate corruption but also to take advantage of it. According to the Mensah Commission, 88 percent of the total employed labor in Ghana could not afford a balanced diet, even if they spent their entire income on food alone. Understandably, therefore, they are inclined to demand gratuities before performing their services. While members of the senior civil service are paid at rates comparable to those in industrialized societies, the salaries of the junior civil servants reflect the levels of production of the local economy. Their resulting resentments and frustrations often tempt them into corruption. The fact that Ghanaians are increasingly aware of the standard of living in Western countries adds to the pressures on them. Those with professional qualifications or foreign training are especially desirous of having the same standard of living as their Western counterparts. Consequently, I. K. Gyasi points out, they feel it necessary to acquire a big car, a television set, a stereo, and "a bevy of fawning women. We need all of them, and our pay is not enough" [*The Ghanaian Times,* Feb. 13, 1970].

The disrespect for regulations or legal requirements is seen as stemming from the colonial period in which the political system was dominated by foreigners. Corruption then was thought to sabotage somehow colonial rule. Thus, most Ghanaians were not unduly disturbed by the 1956 Jibowu Commission findings that the CPP had used the state-run Cocoa Purchasing Company to provide loans and other favors for party supporters and to finance party activities. . . .

With independence came a need for rapid Africanization at a time when an unprecedented burden was being placed on the civil service. The dearth of competent administrators . . . meant that . . . [Nkrumah] had to manage with what was available, regardless of their shortcomings. Otherwise, he would have had to retain many British officials, which would have been politically impossible. . . .

The leaders of the CPP contended that a one-party system would reduce corruption because, to quote the minister of defense under Nkrumah, "when political parties became a feature of our government organization, civil servants lost their traditional impartiality and divided their loyalties between the government and the parties to which they belonged." Moreover, the heavy costs of campaigning, which is a great source of corruption in Western countries, would be unnecessary. "Money, which would otherwise be spent on party functionaries and party organization, would be saved for development projects" [*The Legon Observer*, Aug. 19, 1966]. Of course, the effect of a one-party system was to eliminate one of the most important factors reducing corruption in Western countries: the fear of defeat in a competitive election. . . .

Nkrumah had hoped to build a mass party, such as that of the Soviet Union or China, with himself as a charismatic leader, with his own ideas as a guide to action, and with disciples able to indoctrinate the masses. In reality, however, his associates were bound by nothing more than patronage or fear. "In many cases," Nkrumah admits, "all they were concerned with was taking the places of the former colonial occupiers of their jobs and making the same money as these did in the same social and economic pattern."

What Nkrumah fails to acknowledge was the extent to which he not only encouraged the corruption of his subordinates but also relied upon it. "Nkrumah somehow developed the notion that everybody had his price, and that he could use those whom he bought to further his own ambitions or to flatter and nurture his ego, often at great public expense" [T. P. Omari. *Kwame Nkrumah*. Accra. 1970.]. Those who were most corruptible were thought to be most cooperative. On the other hand, those who resisted these temptations were considered dangerous and, as such, punished. . . .

The Ghanaian concern about corruption, it is here suggested, is an indication of their progressiveness. It arises out of their awareness of the relationship of legality to political development—a relationship established as long ago as the writings of Aristotle. If there is no consciousness of legality, there can hardly be a consciousness of corruption because it assumes some form of legality which is violated. However, from the Ghanaian point of view, their studies of corruption will have been useless if they do not lead to reform. At the roots of corruption they hope to find, if not measures to eradicate it, then the possibility of minimizing it.

IV. ECONOMIC MODERNIZATION

EDITOR'S INTRODUCTION

The economies of the newly independent nations, like their political systems, bear the heavy imprint of their colonial past. All the new nations are engaged in a race to modernize, to close the gap between their former masters, the rich nations, and themselves.

In the early 1960s the goal of closing the gap appeared distant but not impossible. Much of that early optimism has vanished, for reasons which Robert d'A. Shaw of the Overseas Development Council explores in the first selection. As more is learned about the development process, the obstacles appear to loom larger. High on the list is the problem of jobs for the unemployed and the underemployed and, closely related to this, the problem of burgeoning populations. Whereas in the early 1960s industrialization seemed to be the answer to the developing countries' needs, today greater attention is being given to the problem of providing at least a subsistence living for the rural poor. This is the subject of Guy Hunter's piece, which focuses on the African scene.

Countries with a variety of resources stand a better chance of "making it" than those which have inherited one-crop or two-crop economies. Jim Hoagland of the Washington *Post* describes a typical one-crop economy in Africa, that of Senegal.

As the case of Senegal illustrates, how a country manages its resources can sometimes be even more important than the magnitude of the resources. In his second contribution, Jim Hoagland takes a look at Tanzania's Socialist experiment. Following this, the New York *Times* correspondent Thomas A. Johnson describes Nigerianization, and foreign correspondent Michael Wall of *The Economist* staff analyzes Algeria's approach to development.

One of the major worries of the early 1960s—that population growth would soon outstrip food production in the developing world—has been partially assuaged by the phenomenon known as the green revolution, which has made possible an enormous increase in wheat and rice output. The green revolution, however, has produced some undesirable side effects. Some of these are explored by Richard Critchfield of the Washington *Star*.

If the development goals of the newly independent nations are to be achieved, those nations will require, in the opinion of many experts, a major infusion of external aid. The prospects for more development aid are the subject of the final selection, reprinted from *America*.

THE FIRST DEVELOPMENT DECADE [1]

[Ten years after the United Nations General Assembly proclaimed the sixties the Development Decade] the world mood is more somber. The enthusiastic assault on third-world problems has had many successes; but we have also learned that development is a long and gradual process, fraught with difficulties and not attainable merely through the beneficence of the rich countries. Developing countries as a whole seem to have achieved the economic growth target set for the decade: a 5 percent annual increase in their gross national product (GNP). Individual countries, such as Libya, Taiwan, South Korea, Israel and Iran, have achieved sustained rates of growth that are among the highest in history. And the threat that population would outrun the food supply, particularly in India and Pakistan, has largely been averted for the near future, at least.

[1] From *Rethinking Economic Development*, pamphlet by Robert d'A. Shaw, research fellow, Overseas Development Council in Washington, D.C. (Headline Series No. 208) Foreign Policy Association. 345 E. 46th St. New York 10017. '71. p 4-6. Copyright © 1971 by Foreign Policy Association, Inc. Reprinted by permission.

Along with these successes, however, has come evidence of growing malaise with the current approaches to development throughout the world. In the first place, economic growth rates have been very uneven. While some of the smaller countries have performed exceptionally well, vast regions containing the majority of the world's poor have seen little progress. The Indian subcontinent, Indonesia, most of Africa, as well as much of Latin America fall into this category.

At the same time many of the most critical problems of poverty seem to have been growing worse. Population growth continues unchecked and promises a world of at least 6 billion people as we enter the third millennium. And what evidence we have on income distribution from a study done by David Turnham for the Organization for Economic Cooperation and Development (OECD) suggests that it is becoming more unequal in most developing countries. . . . In the meantime, the absolute levels of poverty in the poor countries are appalling. In rural India there are perhaps 200 million people who subsist on less than $1.50 a week each. . . . The Report of the Pearson Commission on International Development stated in 1969:

> In many, if not most of . . . [the developing countries], unemployment is turning into a major social problem and obstacle to development. The failure to create meaningful employment is the most tragic failure of development. All indications are that unemployment and underutilization of human resources have increased in the 1960s, and that the problem will grow even more serious.

Men Without Jobs

All these factors—population, the increasing disparities in incomes between and within countries and the failure to provide employment—have led to an increase in the number of people in the third world who are not participating in development. In the words of Robert S. McNamara, president of the World Bank:

> The cities are filling up and urban unemployment steadily grows. Very probably there is an equal measure of worklessness in

the countryside. The poorest quarter of the population in developing lands risks being left almost entirely behind in the vast transformation of the modern technological society. The "marginal" men, the wretched strugglers for survival on the fringes of farm and city, may already number more than half a billion. By 1980 they will surpass a billion; by 1990, two billion. Can we imagine any human order surviving with so gross a mass of misery piling up at its base?

This phenomenon is a major cause of the disillusionment around the world with the current approach to development. In many developing countries, the pressures of poverty are exacerbating communal tensions and political rivalries. The headlines of the world's newspapers often blazen forth military coups, insurrections and political kidnappings. In the first half of 1971 alone there were successful overthrows of governments in Turkey, Uganda, Argentina and Dahomey, unsuccessful assaults on the governments of Ceylon, Morocco and the Sudan, as well as the devastation of political unity in the world's fifth most populous nation, Pakistan. And all this occurred against a background of terrorism, hijackings and political violence occurring in many other countries. Obviously we cannot directly trace these events to the failure of the development process; nonetheless that failure does seem to have established the preconditions for the upheavals. . . .

"MARGINAL MEN" [2]

We have . . . the emergence of a new phenomenon in the developing world. This is what Mr. McNamara has called the rising incidence of "marginal men"—people who have reached adulthood with no useful role to play in their societies. The products of an unprecedented population explosion due in large part to the success of public health programs the world over, these individuals now face a dearth of

[2] From *Rethinking Economic Development*, pamphlet by Robert d'A. Shaw, research fellow, Overseas Development Council in Washington, D.C. (Headline Series No. 208) Foreign Policy Association. 345 E. 46th St. New York 10017. '71. p 10-13+. Copyright © 1971 by Foreign Policy Association, Inc. Reprinted by permission.

jobs, the most commonly recognized means of providing for themselves and taking part in life around them.

The last director-general of the ILO [International Labour Organization] has given a rough estimate that there may be as many as 75 million people unemployed in the Third World; that is, just about the same number of people as *have* jobs in the United States. Of course, we should note that the problems of measuring unemployment in the poor countries are formidable, and that many of the statistics are little more than informed guesses. But, despite the lack of precise measurement, we can say with certainty that this number of completely unemployed people is only a part of a wider employment problem, whose core is the need to provide families with the means of making a decent livelihood. Many millions of other workers have to take whatever work they can find.

Any traveler to the vacation areas of the poor continents is besieged by hordes of eager baggage carriers, shoe-shine boys and tourist guides—people existing on tips because there is no other work. Millions of workers in these countries subsist on casual labor, while others often work extremely long hours for miserable pittances, reflecting the competition for jobs as well as the shortage of capital and skills. And in the countryside, hundreds of millions of peasants work tiny plots. While they may work very long hours during the harvest season, they often have little to do during the rest of the year. What meager crops they produce bestow on their families a heritage of malnutrition and poverty. Finally, the cities of many developing countries are plagued with petty thieves, beggars and prostitutes, all trying to add to the incomes of their families in the absence of jobs paying decent wages.

The stark facts of poverty dictate that only a small proportion of the population can afford to remain without a job, any kind of job, for long. In an Indian family, where each person lives on less than $6 a month, every member has to take almost whatever work is available, however casual in nature it may be. Since the cushion of social security does not exist, full-time unemployment is almost a luxury that can be indulged in only by those with relatives who have jobs and are prepared to support them.

Furthermore, even those with good jobs are affected by this employment problem, quite apart from the burden of having to support those members of the family who may be without jobs. The bargaining strength of those employed is sapped by the existence of so many willing to take work at almost any wages. And, as a consequence, their jobs are insecure; the workers are dependent on the goodwill of management and are on the defensive against those who might take their work away from them. . . .

In Africa and Asia, . . . [the unemployment pattern is less clear than in Latin America]. Some countries, such as Ceylon, East Pakistan [now Bangladesh], the Philippines and Kenya, have high rates of unemployment in the Western sense; others, notably some of the biggest and poorest, do not. Thus India and Indonesia have recorded rates of unemployment hovering around 1 percent. In these countries, the real problem is not so much one of joblessness, since, as we saw earlier, most people will work at any kind of "job." Rather, concern in these countries lies with the poverty and hopelessness of people who do not have adequate jobs to provide for themselves and their families.

We can, therefore, view the employment problem in some sense as a redefinition of the general problem of poverty itself. Employment is the most important variable that is likely to affect the presence or absence of poverty. Thus, in the final analysis, the objective of development policies should not be just to provide more hours of work, but to create jobs that are productive and that yield enough income for a reasonable standard of living.

If we were to assume the present employment situation in the developing countries will remain static, merely providing enough good jobs for those wanting them would be a formidable task. But the situation is not static. Today, twenty years after the population explosion began in the poor countries, the world is seeing the start of a labor force explosion of unprecedented dimensions. One rather conservative estimate from the ILO has shown that in the decade of the seventies, 225 million additional workers will join the labor forces in the poor countries. This means that, in the course of ten years, the poor countries must create the capital and organizational ability to provide jobs for three times as many workers as there are now in all of Britain, France and West Germany.

Population Growth, Employment and Savings

In the short run, a decline in the rate of population growth will have a profound effect on rates of saving and on the composition of investment. For obvious reasons, families with a large number of children tend to save less than those with fewer. If these savings from smaller families can be channeled into productive investment, then this will create more jobs. At the same time, if each worker has a large number of dependents, relatively larger sums are required for social investment in the forms of schools, housing and other social factors. The society has to provide these facilities, but, given a particular level of expenditure, this means less money to be spent on other items. If there were fewer dependents per worker, some of the investment could be diverted to activities that contribute directly to production, and so could provide higher growth rates and more employment.

Ceylon provides a vivid example of this dilemma. The island has one of the most extensive social welfare systems in the Third World. Education has been free and widespread for over twenty-five years. Today, 77 percent of the population is supposed to be literate and school enrollment rates are over 90 percent for the primary school age group. Medical facilities are also free and widely available so that the average expectation of life is second only to Japan in Asia. Transport was heavily subsidized until July . . . [1971], and each person received one free and one subsidized ration of rice per week. All of this, of course, has been a tremendous drain on the budget and has left too little over for productive investment. As a result economic growth has been very sluggish (probably not exceeding 1 percent per capita a year over the last two decades), and there is heavy unemployment.

THE AFRICAN SCENE [3]

A dual economy, reflecting the contrast between colonial administration and investment on the one hand, and the indigenous economy on the other, was bound to exist in Africa. The early independence policies of industrializing and building a top-quality modern infrastructure, which were reinforced by foreign aid, widened the gap still further, gradually substituting an African elite for a European one. The result has often been described in terms of modern capital cities (surrounded by shack towns), trunk roads, airports, tourist hotels, a few modern factories and at least one superb university structure in each country. The rapid growth of (usually) more modest primary and secondary schools and of the provision of teachers for them has been the biggest contribution of the aided modernizing process to a better balance in society.

The difficulty of escaping from this situation has been underemphasized; perhaps the briefest glance at history will make it more clear. When Europe entered the industrial revolution populations were small and grew at a moderate pace —the highest rate in a decade in Britain was 1.4 percent per annum (1820-1830). There was therefore a good chance of absorbing the extra manpower into rapidly growing industries. Besides, between 1600 and 1900 northern and western Europe conquered or penetrated Canada, the United States, South America, Africa, much of the Near East, India and Burma, Indochina, Malaya, Indonesia, the Philippines, the Pacific islands, Australia and New Zealand—that does not leave much of the rest of the world save for Russia, China

[3] From "The New Africa," article by Guy Hunter, research officer, Overseas Development Institute, London. *Foreign Affairs.* 48:716-20+. Jl. '70. Excerpted by permission from *Foreign Affairs,* July 1970. Copyright © 1970 by the Council on Foreign Relations, Inc., New York.

and Japan. The growing industrial nations had a decisive technological superiority. It was therefore not necessary for British industry to await the expansion of consumer demand within the nation's own agricultural community, for the markets of a conquered world were open. Public expenditure on education and social services was small (primary education did not become universal until the 1880s in Britain, long after the main technical expansion had taken place). Nationhood had been established for centuries.

Contrast with this story that of Africa. Population growth has preceded industrial development, and at 2.5 to 3 percent per annum. There is no new world to expand into; there is no technical superiority to wield in existing markets; industry must wait upon the growth of consumer demand from among the vast bulk of rural population—in the 1960s Tanzania was classified as 95 percent rural, 5 percent urban; education and social services have come before industrial development on a large scale; national unity is barely ten years old.

This list of contrasts is, to my mind, staggering. It faces Africa, and to a lesser degree most other developing countries, with a situation which is unique in modern history. With no large external market for manufactures, and without the ability of a Britain or a Switzerland to import raw materials, apply special skills and reexport them, the foundation of African economies had to be laid in primary production—lucky were those with oil or copper—using agricultural or mineral exports to purchase equipment for industry. But industry in turn was limited to the internal market, and low productivity and low incomes in the massive agricultural sector narrowly limited chances for industrial expansion or for the growth of small-scale processing, commerce, distributive and technical services from which a more solid economy could grow. The small modern sector typically was burdened with overvalued exchange rates (favoring imports of sophisticated machinery and elite consumption goods), excessively high differentials between urban and rural earnings, a stagnant agriculture and a growing menace of unemployment. The mineral-rich countries (Zambia, Nigeria and the oil countries of North Africa) find it even harder to unify the high-reward mining economy with the subsistence hinterland.

It is this situation, not confined to Africa, which has led to rich cash-crop exports alongside miserable subsistence agriculture and to the paradox of widespread malnutrition and even hunger alongside complaints of limited demand for agricultural output. . . .

In short, the attempt to industrialize from the top downward by borrowing sophisticated techniques, while 60 to 70 percent of the population remained in a stagnant rural economy, represents an attempt to enter the twentieth-century world industrial economy before the domestic foundations have been properly laid. The worst symptom is unemployment, which will be the dominant problem of Africa in the 1970s; the way on is—*"reculer pour mieux sauter"* [step back, the better to leap forward]—to return to a really thorough development of the traditional agricultural sector, accompanied by a development of the processing, supply and consumer goods industries and services which a successful and modernized agriculture demands. . . .

These grim calculations have been accepted only slowly. The first tendency in Africa, under the pressure of the foreign exchange drain in the modern sector, was to reemphasize export crops, until markets began to be filled and the threat of unemployment sharpened. The second main response was to create very expensive settlement schemes; East and West Nigeria, Tanzania and Kenya have felt very sharply the cost and the small economic result (although in Kenya the political gain was worth the cost). Only in the last year or two has real attention moved to enriching, diversifying and commercializing internal food production, with its possible gains not only in nutrition but, above all, in employment. Hopefully, a highly intensive agriculture, with doubled farm incomes, could create a hum of construction as well as commercial, distributive, processing and servicing activity which could bring a substantial volume of wasted human and technical potential into productivity and start to build the economy from below.

The idea of the green revolution and the importance of agriculture are beginning to grow all over the developing world, and there have been remarkable successes in India, Pakistan, Taiwan, Mexico and at scattered points in Africa and Latin America. But there is still a long way to go before statements about the priority of the agricultural sector are borne out by priorities in resource allocation: in physical investment, personnel, training, education, market incentives. How many countries still are content with one field extension officer to 1,500 or 2,000 farming families? Indeed, in Mexico and in India there are clear dangers that the green revolution will simply add a small group of the larger and more powerful farmers to the modern sector, leaving the other three quarters of the rural economy relatively worse off. . . .

Science—the Accelerator

If we look at the record of African countries over the last ten years, we thus see them seeking desperately to contain the demands of economic growth and alien technical change within a social and political structure party borrowed, partly invented, seldom reinforced by indigenous tradition. Alas, the tools chosen for this process, far from being closely adapted to local circumstances and stages of growth, have usually been "blanket" choices—of cooperatives, district commissioners, universities, development corporations or whatever—largely reflecting ideology, or fashion, or the home practice of the consultant who advises. In the 1970s the technical means of agricultural advance in the tropics will at last be widely available: now far more thought is needed on the administrative and institutional patterns through which the contribution of science—the one great accelerator—can be made effective in the unique combination of seventeenth century society and twentieth century technique.

SENEGAL: PEASANTS' REVOLT [4]

A modest peasants' revolt, carried out by farmers refusing to grow and market the lowly peanut, is forcing major concessions out of the government of the prodigal city slickers who run this West African country.

Both Senegal, which was once the pampered child of the French colonial family, and the peanut which provides 30 percent of Senegal's export earnings, have fallen on hard times recently.

Dissatisfied with government policies and declining price support, suspecting official corruption and plagued by bad weather, Senegal's peasants have accomplished their own, effective work stoppage.

In the process they have cut production of the vital peanut crop in half, and put a painful economic squeeze on a government addicted to living beyond its meager means.

"The peasants have been paying the bills for independence, as they have all over Africa," said one experienced Western observer in Dakar. "They have found out how expensive it is, and I think they have had enough of seeing their real income fall every year."

The agricultural unrest and the government's belated attempts to deal with it have important implications for the rest of this continent and perhaps for the developing world.

As in Senegal, 90 percent of Africa's population are peasants—that is, they live off what they can grow on the land, and the little cash they obtain comes from crops they can sell.

The French, who began their penetration of this South Dakota-sized nation on the western bulge of Africa, developed the arid, infertile interior of Senegal exclusively for peanut production, to obtain cooking oil.

This gave Senegal the classic colonial economy, chained to one crop that was highly vulnerable to world price fluctuations.

[4] From article, "Peasant Revolt Cuts Senegal's Vital Peanut Crop," by Jim Hoagland, staff correspondent. Washington *Post.* p A 29-30. Ag. 9, '70. Copyright © 1972 by The Washington Post. Reprinted by permission.

They also made Dakar the administrative and industrial capital for all of French West Africa, and used the Senegalese as their African administrators throughout their territories. The country prospered and developed especially strong cultural links to France.

Independence a Blow

Independence in 1960 came as something of a blow. . . . French West Africa was transformed into eight independent countries, all with their own tariff barriers and civil services.

Senegal's market shrank from 20 million to its own population of 3.5 million. The bloated civil service in Dakar continued to administer but had nothing to administer.

Bolstered by French budgetary aid and subsidies for the peanut crop, the Senegalese government made no austerity moves to reflect the new situation.

Expensive imports continued to eat up the country's foreign-exchange earnings. The government ordered big new buildings for the administrators, whose salaries take up over 40 percent of the national budget, and urged the farmers to plant more peanuts to pay for all this.

Trouble After 1966

Trouble began after the 1966 crop, which produced a record one million tons. Then the subsidy and world market price for peanuts fell, and producers found their income shrinking. Two years of bad weather followed, and by 1969 the crop was down to 623,000 tons and Senegal's budget deficit was up to $20 million.

Blaming external factors, the government predicted production would rise, and planned for 1.2 million tons. Last year [1969], Senegal had good weather and the world market price for peanuts rose sharply. The result: Senegal produced one of its worst crops in history with about 570,000 tons being sold.

This made it clear that more than weather was inhibiting production. Without the excuse of weather to hide behind, even officials in Dakar have begun to speak, with some alarm, of the "peasants' malaise" that afflicts the countryside.

"There has been a certain mistrust by the peasants of some of our agricultural policies," said Senegal's newly named prime minister, Abdou Diouf, in an interview. . . . "The peasants have lost confidence in certain promises that were made. We must restore that confidence."

Peanut Smuggling

Many of the peanuts that were grown were smuggled into the Gambia, a neighboring enclave of a country where buyers paid slightly higher prices—and, more importantly, paid cash on the spot.

The smuggling has been a highly organized affair with trucks and boats loaded with peanuts rolling across the poorly policed border. While Senegal was posting bad yields, the Gambia was producing near record "harvests" every year. At one point, Senegal had to buy back from Gambia several thousand tons of the smuggled peanuts in order to fill contractual obligations.

As is often the case, the farmers' grievances center around money.

While peanuts are selling at about 16 West African francs a pound on the open market, the government has pegged the price paid to farmers by the government-controlled cooperative at 8 francs. (One West African franc is equal to about three tenths of a US cent.)

In fact, by the time the money got to the farmer, it had been whittled away to 6 francs a pound, and no one could really explain what had happened to the 2 missing francs. Also, the government deducted from the farmers' proceeds costs for fertilizer and seeds he had been required to buy.

The difference between the market price and cooperative price was supposed to go into a stabilization fund that would tide the farmers over in bad years. But official sources now admit that much of the fund has been eaten up by government expenses, and some of it has just disappeared.

The peasants were also upset about having to take IOUs from the cooperatives when the crops were sold. The pledges were redeemed a few months later, but in the meantime, speculators had moved in and bought up many of the IOUs at a discount, and the farmers' profits had shrunk to nil.

As a result, the farmers have become agricultural dropouts and the country's trade deficit has tripled within a year. The shock waves have forced the government to adopt what some observers think is a more realistic approach to the peasants, who have been largely ignored by the city-bound elite.

The peasants' malaise is credited with being a major factor in President Leopold S. Senghor's streamlining of his government . . . [in 1970] and bringing in Abdou Diouf as his new prime minister.

Noted as a hard-working, no-nonsense administrator, the thirty-five-year-old Diouf lists the solving of the peasants' problems (he thinks *malaise* is too strong a word) as his first priority.

Diversification

Asserting that Senegal was making large gains in its effort to escape from the tyranny of the peanut by diversifying into crops like rice, cotton and millet, Diouf said the government was going to immediately refund one of the missing francs per pound to the farmers on . . . [the 1969] crop, and said that he would announce shortly higher prices "that will be a very happy surprise for the peasant" for . . . [the 1970] crop, which is being planted now.

In a detailed and surprisingly frank analysis, Diouf indicated that the falling production had forced the government to realize that much of its agricultural program was a failure and had to be overhauled.

He criticized some of the officials of the cooperatives, and hinted that some of the rumors of corruption may be justified. There was a lack of democracy inside the cooperatives, he added, "and the peasant did not feel it was his thing.

"In the future, we will let him choose whether or not to belong to the cooperative, to use fertilizer and other materials. Our first task is to open a dialogue with the peasant and to regain his confidence."

This new-found willingness to grapple with Senegal's agricultural problems does not, of course, guarantee that they will be solved. Some observers point out that Senegal, with its surfeit of trained administrators, is already knee-deep in good plans that cannot be implemented.

The government may also run into serious opposition if it goes beyond mere superficial agricultural reform. The mass of the peasants, and much of the peanut crop, are controlled by a rural oligarchy headed by Islamic chieftains known as marabouts, who have cooperated with agriculture reform only when it coincides with their own interests. Much of Senghor's political support is derived from the marabouts, so he is not likely to tread on their toes.

He must also be careful not to upset the French, who still have a major interest in the peanut crop.

But for the moment, at least, the peasants of Senegal do seem to have hammered a better deal out of the government, along with a recognition that they too have a stake in the country's benefits.

TANZANIA: SOCIALIST EXPERIMENT [5]

The fate of an ambitious attempt to transform poverty-stricken and backward rural areas of Africa into self-governing Socialist communes rides on a desperate gamble being made in the dusty, famine-swept hills of central Tanzania. . . . The government has persuaded more than 41,000 families, mostly seminomadic Wagogo tribesmen, to leave the barren plains they usually inhabit and settle in Ujamaa villages around the town of Dodoma.

This spectacular movement of population has given Tanzania's intellectually inclined president, Julius K. Nyerere, his first real opportunity to show that *Ujamaa*—a Swahili

[5] From article, "A Time of Testing For Nyerere's Socialist Vision," by Jim Hoagland, staff correspondent. Washington *Post.* p B 5. Ap. 9, '72. Copyright © 1972 by The Washington Post. Reprinted by permission.

word usually translated as "familyhood"—is more than a theory.

Even some of Nyerere's most ardent admirers are apprehensive about the chances for the Dodoma experiment. The Wagogo, among the poorest and most backward people of this East African nation of thirteeen million farmers, are not flocking to the Ujamaa villages out of a yearning for socialism, but out of desperation.

Two successive droughts have brought them to the point of famine. "They have come, in numbers far greater than we expected, because they have been promised water," said one of Nyerere's principal advisers. "We must now try to take advantage of that situation."

"Perhaps the people do not understand what *Ujamaa* is," said another Ujamaa theorist who has worked in the Dodoma region. "But we have told the Wagogo that *Ujamaa* will provide them good things, which is the ultimate truth of socialism. Someday they will understand."

The success of Nyerere's most important political idea thus depends on the efforts of a group of Tanzania's least productive and most poorly educated people, who have resettled on poor land. And this fact points up what may be an even larger difficulty for *Ujamaa* in the future.

Nyerere has clearly been unable to convince more successful farmers—that is, more aggressive, better educated and technically progressive ones—that *Ujamaa* has anything to offer them as members of Tanzania's small population of "haves."

"Our people here often say the government is just trying to spread poverty," said one hard-working and moderately well-off farmer in the West Kilimanjaro area of Tanzania. "They want us to share with others who do not want to work."

An African Problem

The jarring collision of the goals of scientific socialism and the world of the African peasant is also stirring opposition to Nyerere's policies on the Tanzanian left. Radicals predict failure for the attempt to seduce the Wagogo into socialism and blame Nyerere for being unrealistic and too soft on the *kulaks*—the Russian word for rich peasants, which is in vogue here.

"You can only collectivize peasants through force," an expatriate lecturer at the University of Dar es Salaam argued recently. "To talk about doing it through gentle persuasion is to ignore all the lessons of socialism."

The success or failure of *Ujamaa* in Tanzania is important for all of sub-Sahara Africa, where more than 80 percent of the 200 million population are peasants. Many of them work small plots of land for corn or yams to eat and sometimes earn a few dollars a year doing agricultural work for others.

It is a hard life. Schools, roads and hospitals are nonexistent in many of these rural areas. Since independence, there has been a steady stream of peasants quitting the countryside to pour into Africa's slum-ridden cities, despite there being no work for them there.

This urban drift accentuates another great problem, to which less attention has been devoted. African farmers are producing less food per head each year, as productivity remains static and population increases. Africa is less able to feed itself with each passing year.

Productivity increases have for the most part been in crops grown for sale abroad, such as coffee, tea and cotton. This reflects both the agricultural patterns developed under colonialism and the desire of independent governments to export crops and build up foreign reserves—which then get spent on urban areas.

The broad pattern so far has been the same across Africa, whether in Socialist Tanzania or capitalist Ivory Coast. Significantly, the agricultural production gains scored are almost entirely the result of increased acreage, not yield.

Rural development has been fastened on by almost all of Africa's governments as the answer to these problems. To date, however, rural development has remained an empty political promise in most countries, which do not have enough money, trained manpower or often even the desire to implement it.

The countries that are active in the countryside tend to present rural development as the spread of efficient small-holder farming, which will raise the standards of living of those willing to work hard.

In Kenya, Ghana, the Ivory Coast, Malawi and a few other countries, local "entrepreneurs" who use fertilizer, insecticides or perhaps tractors to make a profit are held up as models for other peasants. This encourages the growth of cash crop farming at the expense of food.

Only Tanzania has proposed and begun to put into effect a radical alternative. *Ujamaa* springs at least partly from Nyerere's long association with Fabian socialism, although he prefers to emphasize its African aspects.

About 95 percent of Tanzania's population lives in rural areas. Once a German colony and then a British trust territory before achieving independence in 1961, Tanzania is one of Africa's least developed countries, producing cotton, coffee, sisal and a few other crops.

The Ujamaa village has often been termed Africa's equivalent of the Chinese agricultural commune or the Israeli kibbutz, comparisons that are only partly valid.

Israeli aid experts who have studied the theory of *Ujamaa* note, for example, that the kibbutz movement was able to draw on educated and skilled people who were willing to give up much in a return to nature. *Ujamaa* is an attempt to develop managerial skills in peasants, without the benefit of the profit motive. . . .

The Poorest Respond

The building of Nyerere's new rural society is based on two options. One is for officials to convince existing villages to give up individual effort and convert to collective and Socialist principles.

There have been relatively few successful Ujamaa villages formed in this way, officials say. The government has had to depend on regrouping scattered farmers on new land, with promises of wells, clinics, schools and other benefits in return for the peasants' promise to abide by Ujamaa.

"We have had success in areas where land is not highly valued, where there is no land shortage and no permanent crops," said R. S. Juma, the government's coordinator of Ujamaa villages. "In areas where there is a higher degree of socioeconomic development, you have fewer Ujamaa villages."

Charting Ujamaa village concentrations bears out Juma's point. They are clustered in poor, have-not areas, such as southern Tanzania and Dodoma, while the progressive Chagga tribesmen around Mt. Kilimanjaro have refused to take *Ujamaa* seriously.

The government insists that force is not used in getting peasants to move into villages. The documented cases of overzealous local officials rounding up people and making them become *Wajamaa,* as village residents are termed, are exceptions to policy, officials say.

These officials also attempt to discount the increasing reports of failures of already established villages, as disappointed residents who have not received the health clinics or schools they were promised desert *Ujamaa* and return to their former homes.

Some cases of villages failing have been documented, but for the most part the government attempts to keep them from coming to light. Nyerere, normally an open-minded man, refuses to listen to reports of failure on *Ujamaa,* highly reliable sources indicate. Outsiders are not permitted to visit Ujamaa villages without special government permission.

Increasing internal difficulty may account for what appears to be a tightening by the government of access to Ujamaa villages in recent weeks, after a previous policy of shepherding visitors to a few villages that Nyerere in a candid moment once called showcases.

"We don't want the people to be disturbed by tourists all the time," Tanzania's director of information, A. A. Riyami, explained. He added, however, that journalists had always received permission to visit villages in the past. But nearly one month later, after repeated requests, Riyami said permission could not be granted now for this correspondent to visit any Ujamaa villages. He would not elaborate. . . .

$460 a Year

For Nyerere; one of the key features of rural familyhood is arresting the spread of rural capitalism, which he claims was largely unknown to traditional African society before the colonialists introduced the cash economy into farming.

In other areas, such as Latin America, the phrase rural capitalists might conjure up the image of wealthy absentee landlords controlling many plantations and workers.

But outside Ethiopia, such situations are rare in Africa, where land is often held communally. In a number of countries there are great tracts of vacant land. One of Nyerere's first acts as president was to assert that all land belonged to the state. Only now has this begun to produce conflicts with those tribes who have practiced individual land ownership.

In Tanzanian terms, the "rich peasant" who is the enemy of socialism nets about $460 a year from crop sales and hires two workmen to help him with three acres of cotton or coffee, according to examples Nyerere has given in his writings and speeches.

The most advanced farmers in Tanzania, the Chagga, appear to feel that they have been singled out as counterrevolutionaries because of their success.

The Chagga, who have a tradition of individual ownership in their fertile but overcrowded Kilimanjaro area, have developed small but profitable coffee farms, formed one of Africa's best marketing cooperatives, and were among the first in Tanzania to build their own schools and strive to send their children to college.

They are in essence the kind of farmers that other African countries urge their rural populations to emulate, and to whom development credit and technical help is usually funneled. Here, however, they have been bluntly told that they will not receive government help unless they adopt *Ujamaa*. Thus far, they have chosen to go it alone, and appear to be still prospering more than other groups in Tanzania.

"A lot of research will be required before we can say what the best path is for bringing *Ujamaa* into such areas," R. S. Juma said when asked about the Chagga. "We don't have a blanket formula for the whole country."

"NIGERIANIZATION" [6]

Nigeria is making bold moves toward controlling her own economy—for the first time.

Such words as *indigenization* and *Nigerianization* are most often used here to describe these attempts.

While their meanings are not always clearly expressed, many Nigerians are certain that both spell out a future when the greatest share of this nation's potential wealth will go to Nigerians.

They insist that both terms really mean reversing of conditions disclosed by the federal Industrial Survey of Nigeria 1968 that showed non-Nigerians controlled 70 percent of the nation's 625 largest manufacturing establishments.

In addition, the Central Bank of Nigeria's *Economic and Financial Review* for 1967-1968 showed that British concerns controlled 56 percent of Nigeria's fixed foreign assets and that American companies controlled 20 percent. Nigerians controlled less than 6 percent.

Nigerian Managers Required

The Nigerian Enterprises Promotion Decree, 1972, issued ... [in] February, has been the most public of the indigeniza-

[6] From "Nigeria Moves Boldly to Gain Control of Her Economy," article by Thomas A. Johnson, staff correspondent. New York *Times*. p 27+. S. 2, '72. © 1972 by The New York Times Company. Reprinted by permission.

tion moves. It stated that as of March 31, 1974, some fifty-five categories of business enterprises, services and trades would be operated solely by Nigerians or Africans.

Bank loans are to be provided, the decree stated, to Nigerian businessmen who seek to buy out foreigners now engaged in such enterprises.

Major expatriate-owned concerns not affected by the decree must Nigerianize a percentage of their management positions. In addition, these concerns—many are international, multimillion dollar operations—are required to allow Nigerians to purchase at least a 40 percent ownership.

"The big difference today is that we are on much happier grounds for bargaining, and it is getting better and better for us," said Dr. J. E. Adetoro, Nigeria's commissioner of industries. . . .

The happier grounds, he added, are directly above great pools of crude oil.

"We have recently struck new oil fields," Mr. Adetoro said, "and it appears we are sitting on a huge lake of oil."

And it is oil—a two-million-barrel-a-day production was predicted by the *Standard Bank Review* . . . [in] February [1972]—that has lessened this generally underdeveloped nation's need for foreign investments.

At the same time the oil revenues have permitted Nigeria's 62 million citizens to greatly increase their role as consumers.

Writing for the Nigerian *Bulletin of Foreign Affairs,* a British economics writer, Andrew C. E. Hiton, contended that foreign investors would not quit Nigeria because they "cannot afford to be excluded from a market which, it has been estimated (by Nigeria's Ministry of Development and Reconstruction), will grow at over 10 percent per annum."

Mr. Adetoro said there had been no lessening of foreign companies' wanting to come into Nigeria, and he reported an expansion of Nigerian trade talks with several nations, including the United States, Scotland, Italy, Britain, the Soviet Union and China. He said Nigeria did not intend to chase expatriate business out of the country. . . .

One of the biggest helps for the indigenization and Nigerianization processes came when Chief Simeon Adebo, the Nigerian under secretary-general to the United Nations, announced earlier this summer [1972] that he would resign and become a consultant on research and training to the multi-million-dollar, multinational United Africa Company Amalgamation.

During a recent talk in Lagos, Mr. Adebo, who had been the executive director of the UN's Institute for Training and Research, said he left the United Nations because "I am anxious to join the struggle for the salvation of this country, whether in or out of government."

He continued, "The United Africa Company does intend to indigenize. I have no higher interest than to apply myself in this way to the betterment of this country."

ALGERIA'S DEVELOPMENT GOALS [7]

Algeria has gone all out for industrialization on a centrally controlled Socialist pattern. The aim is to achieve complete economic independence, as the government firmly rejects the idea that Algeria should remain a supplier of cheap raw materials and labor for the developed countries and an importer of their manufactured goods. The government has also rejected the theory that light industries should be developed first so as to provide a ready market for the products of heavy industries. After taking power in 1965, the Boumedienne government drew up two development plans covering 1966-1969 and 1970-1974. These were tied to the establishment and expansion of heavy and basic industries.

The government further reasoned that this policy could not be carried out unless the state controlled all sectors of economic activity by holding all the levers of capital invest-

[7] From article, "Maghreb; A Survey," by Michael Wall, foreign correspondent, in collaboration with Sue Dearden. *Economist* (London). 242:survey p 12-14. Mr. 11, '72. Reprinted by permission.

ment. And, following an orthodox Socialist line, the planners went on to argue that as the development of heavy industry had to be on a large scale to be at all viable, the country's economy had to be geared to compete in foreign markets. So all industrial processes had to be of the kind that makes the maximum use of capital and the minimum use of labor. The manufacture of consumer goods, the expansion of the service industries and the revival of the agricultural sector through the use of fertilizers, tractors and machinery was thus firmly put into second place. From such reasoning has flowed the doctrine of nationalization.

Algeria's hydrocarbons, oil and natural gas, are the base on which the economy is being built. Their control by the state at all stages from exploration to marketing was, therefore, seen as essential to the government's policy. But this required trained personnel. The task of training Algerians to run their own industries started in 1964 with the establishment of the African Centre for Hydrocarbons and Textiles for training engineers and technicians. By . . . [1973] it will have 3,000 pupils. In 1965 the Algerian Petroleum Institute was opened for training skilled workers and foremen and since then technical institutes have been set up in several large towns. By the end of 1973 it is estimated that there will be over 10,700 trained Algerians at work in the hydrocarbon industries. . . .

Franco-Algerian Relations

The story of Franco-Algerian relations between the signing of agreements on the exploitation of Algerian oil and gas in July 1965 and the crisis of February 1971 is long, complicated and punctuated by accusations and recriminations. In brief, the Algerians came to believe that the French were not spending enough on exploration and were limiting production to suit the economic interests of France while at the same time they were benefiting from financial concessions on royalties and taxes. Negotiations to modify the 1965 agreements dragged on for almost two years until on February 24, 1971, the Algerian government lost patience and announced that it had raised its participation in all French oil companies to 51 percent and had nationalized the natural gas fields and all pipelines on national territory. On April 12, 1971, the government raised the posted prices of Algerian oil to the level agreed at the Tripoli conference of April 2nd and brought the tax system into line with that operated by the Organization of Petroleum Exporting Countries.

The French accused the Algerians of breaking the 1965 agreement by acting while negotiations were going on. They placed an embargo on Algerian oil. It was met by an Algerian embargo on French imports. In order to preserve foreign exchange and offset the effects of the oil embargo the Algerians were called upon by the government to face a year of austerity. The import of a great deal of the capital equipment needed for the industrialization program was delayed and for once the inefficiency and obstinacy of the Algerian customs department served some purpose, if only a political one. Algerian oil production fell by two thirds and it was not until the end of . . . [1971] when agreement with the second of the two major French groups was finally reached, that the former production rate of 50 metric tons a year was fully restored. The Algerians claim that the financial loss incurred has been made up by the higher prices. . . .

The dispute between Algeria and France over oil has thrown the current four-year development plan awry. The 9 percent cumulative annual increase in gross national product envisaged in this plan was not reached . . . [in 1971]: it was nearer 6 percent. Nevertheless, the Algerians still hope that . . . [in 1972] 94 development projects will come into production. . . .

Private Industry

The private industrialist is the most nervous individual in Algeria today. He fears that even if the government does not nationalize his enterprise he will be squeezed out by other means so as to leave the field open for publicly owned concerns. The government maintains that there is a place for private enterprise in the nonbasic industries and indeed recognize₅ that competition does something to keep the public sector on its toes. But there are occasional barbed comments in the controlled press, for instance about the private sector being able to manufacture at lower prices because it does not spend so much on research. Such comments do nothing to encourage the private investor to extend his operations. In all, the private sector is small: 80 percent of the nonhydrocarbon industry is owned and managed by the government.

Foreign firms are deeply involved in the development program. Their operations are, in the main, on a turnkey basis. They plan, build and equip the plant, factory or pipeline and help train the Algerians to operate it. They pull out when the operation can be left entirely to the Algerians. Apart from the El Hadjar steelworks, which is being constructed by the Russians (the Italians are putting in the hot-rolling mills and the Austrians the cold), the major contracts have gone to Japanese, American, German, British, Italian, French and Austrian firms, for advanced technology carries greater weight in Algeria than any political considerations. . . .

Foreign contractors, including British ones, cannot but be interested in the pace of economic development that the Algerians are hoping to achieve. But, like some Algerians themselves, they must wonder whether too much is being planned and done too quickly. It is easy to trip over one's own feet if one runs at a headlong pace, particularly when the whole economic apparatus is so rigidly controlled.

PUNJAB, BENGAL & THE GREEN REVOLUTION [8]

Indira Gandhi has changed the political map of the Indian subcontinent, but she has not changed the villagers of Bengal and the Punjab nor the way they grow their food. The emergence of Bangladesh as a separate country has been widely interpreted as the beginning of a three-way power

[8] From article by Richard Critchfield, member of editorial staff of Washington *Star. Nation.* 214:134-8. Ja. 31, '72. Reprinted by permission.

struggle for southern Asia, with the Russians the winners of the first round and the Chinese and the Americans the losers. It can also be seen, perhaps more realistically, as the most dramatic episode thus far in a slide toward social chaos and savage struggles to hold or seize in both Bengal and the Punjab resources that have been made even scarcer by the complex forces of overpopulation, cultural uprooting and rapid agricultural change.

The triggering mechanism seems to have been the successful adoption in the past five years of American farm technology in northern India and Pakistan. The newly introduced dwarf, short-stemmed wheat and rice can triple harvests since they can be heavily fertilized with nitrogen without collapsing under the weight of the heads. These new strains have brought both India and Pakistan close to self-sufficiency in food for the first time in thirty years [Since this article was written, India's worst drought in a decade sharply curtailed food grain production.—Ed.] but because of a lack of social leveling, both between the region of the Punjab and Bengal, and between the rural rich and poor within each region, it has caused a series of political explosions which are only beginning. . . .

The Punjab

Despite its rivers, the Punjab receives only five to fifteen inches of rainfall a year. The British irrigated this virtual desert with canals which, by the 1930s served 12.4 million acres. Punjabis were colonized by the British on twenty-five-acre farms and the Punjab became the breadbasket of India. But its population rose 50 percent within a generation and by World War II the region had an average grain surplus of only 5 percent. The Punjab was sinking back toward stagnation and subsistence farming when, along with Bengal, it was the scene of the partition holocaust of 1947, six million Punjabis and Bengalis being uprooted and another million dying in the exchange of populations.

The restoration of the Punjab's agriculture began in the 1950s when the Indian and Pakistani governments both invested heavily in massive hydroelectric projects, introduced rural electrification and subsidized the sinking of hundreds of thousands of tube wells. The truly spectacular transformation, with the new seeds, heavy use of nitrogen fertilizer, tractors, threshing machines and combines giving the Punjab a per acre wheat output nine times higher than that of Kansas, has come only in the last five years, and has somehow escaped general attention.

Bengal's Rural Decline

The decline of Bengali agriculture and disintegration of the Bengali village began, as in Punjab, in the 1940s, but it has never been arrested. The problem has not been too little water but too much. The floodwaters of the Ganges and the Brahmaputra are two and a half times greater than those of the Mississippi and the Missouri; some 60 percent of the region goes under water during the summer monsoon.

In some of Bengal's most densely populated districts, such as Noahkhali and Comila, a steady regression in methods of cultivation has been going on now for two generations. No Bengali landholding of less than 1.5 acres can support a pair of bullocks, and the average farm size of 1.7 acres conceals the reality that half the holdings are less than half an acre. Bengal has therefore undergone a steady retreat from oxen-pulled plows to primitive hand hoes, an agricultural revolution in reverse. The psychological effect of such dense overcrowding and technological regression has never been fully studied, but Noahkhali will be remembered as the scene of Mahatma Gandhi's last pilgrimage; he went there hoping to prevent a slaughter of Moslems and Hindus that, together with similar fighting in the Punjab, cost one million lives. . . .

In both the eastern and western halves of Bengal during the past five years there has been a steady growth of movements by dispossessed peasants, who lack bullocks, money, land or hope, to seize land by force. These Naxalite gangs, named after the village where the land-grab movement began, roam about, killing, looting and condemning landlords by "people's courts" on the old Chinese pattern. Until recently, they defined a *landlord* as a peasant with more than five acres. Now the standard is down to three acres. . . .

Resentment by East Bengalis of Punjabi rule has been so open and longstanding that it is sometimes asked why former President Yahya Khan agreed . . . [in 1971] to hold Pakistan's first general elections in its twenty-three-year history, since it seemed inevitable that the Bengalis would make autonomy the issue. . . .

Green Revolution

Between 1967 and the eve of the Bengali war, the Pakistani Punjab doubled its wheat harvest in the most spectacular advance in grain production in human history. A record rice harvest also brought Pakistan into the market as an exporter. Across the frontier, India did almost as well, its wheat production climbing 50 percent between 1965 and 1969. . . .

In a purely technological sense, the transformation of the Punjab's wheat production was a great success story. Together with Ayub Khan's policy of giving private enterprise its head, it put Pakistan in seventh place, just after Spain, in the rate of growth of its gross national production. . . . [In 1971] the dwarf wheat was planted on 10 million of Pakistan's 15 million irrigated acres; seventy thousand tractors, seven thousand threshing machines and more than one hundred combines have appeared in just the last two to three years in the Punjabi fields.

As early as 1969 I heard predictions at World Bank headquarters in Washington that agricultural success in the Punjab, coming at the same time as continued rural decline in Bengal, would contribute significantly to the breakup of Pakistan, especially as average incomes in the western wing had abruptly risen two-thirds higher than in Bengal.

The fall of Ayub Khan's government, after weeks of urban rioting by uprooted landless laborers and small farmers, first revealed that the modernization of agriculture in the Punjab had not only sharply increased food production but also the number of unemployed peasants. The negative effect of the new methods on the poorer rural classes was more severe on the Pakistani side of the frontier, where the land ownership ceiling was 250 acres; it was 30 acres in the Indian Punjab. Pakistani government statistics claimed that only 15,000 farmers owned holdings larger than 150 acres, but did not emphasize that a great many of these properties were vast estates of 1,000 to 1,500 acres. One large landowner, who had 1,500 acres of irrigated wheat, told me . . . [in 1971] that he had cleared a net profit of more than $100,000 on his last crop. While there had been some land reform under Ayub Khan, it clearly had not gone far enough. . . .

The Future

If India is to be helped to survive as an open society, the place to start is Bangladesh. If the Indians, with Russian support, can restore some semblance of political stability there, massive economic and technical assistance for agriculture ought to be provided by the United States. One possibility would be to develop a new high-yield floating rice, and researchers are already at work. Another would be to get the annual floods of the Ganges and Brahmaputra under control, so that the already available varieties of high-yield dwarf rice could be widely planted. . . .

A massive engineering project is needed, to include the construction of enormous embankments and irrigation systems, and with them an extension service to train Bengali peasants in modern methods of rice cultivation. . . .

In most poor Asian countries the great race has been to see whether industrial employment, with its promise of a decent life, can keep pace with the growth of urbanization, as more and more peasants are uprooted from the overpopulated villages. In Bangladesh, this race has never even been run, since the country's shifting waterways and the lack of any real infrastructure of road and rail communications are serious drawbacks to industrialization. The solution for the 77 million East Bengalis—assuming that those now in West Bengal come home again—must lie in agriculture. The Russians and Indians lack the technology. Although Mrs. Gandhi has talked much of self-reliance and the lack of need for substantial US assistance, if there is any hope for Bangladesh—and indeed for India—the Americans must offer it.

DEVELOPMENT: SOME MISSING LINKS [9]

Most developed nations have accepted 1 percent of their gross national product as the minimum norm determining the extent of their economic assistance to the underdeveloped world. Implementation of that theory, though, has left much to be desired. That, at any rate, is the judgment of the Organization for Economic Cooperation and Development. And OECD's most recent annual report should be of particular interest to Americans. For the first time, the United States has fallen so far behind fellow members of the aid-donors' club that it now ranks last in a field of sixteen. Believe it or not, leading the pack is Portugal, which . . . [in 1970] contributed 2 percent of its GNP for economic assistance abroad.

Meanwhile, the United States has been having a hard time keeping on the heels of Canada. Each is contributing at the moment something less than one half of 1 percent of GNP. Britain, Norway, Sweden, Japan, Australia, Austria and Switzerland range from close to 1 percent down to 0.6 percent. At the other end of the spectrum, the Netherlands is behind Portugal with 1.35 percent; West Germany with 1.34; France with 1.25; Denmark and Belgium with 1.15; and Italy with a tinier fraction above the 1 percent norm.

The actual amount of aid, however, is not the only issue raised by the OECD. The content of aid, the report points out, is equally important. It therefore raises the question whether the aid-giving nations have sufficiently pondered their approaches to economic development abroad. Has not concentration on an economic growth rate been a mistake? What about employment, education, income distribution?

The so-called green revolution, for example, was supposed to be one answer to the problems of the underdeveloped world. Indeed, in the face of a population growth of 2.6 percent compared to the 2 percent of the previous decade, concern for agricultural output made a certain amount of sense. And yet the newly discovered strains of wheat and rice have not at all resulted in the looked-for revolution. If anything, they have created more economic problems.

Burma is the latest country to have revealed signs of being victimized by "miracle rice." At one time the largest exporter of rice in Southeast Asia, Burma's surplus is today virtually unsellable abroad, mainly because of the success of miracle rice among former customers. Sooner or later, the phenomenon that is growing more and more common throughout Asia, the population influx from rural agricultural to urban areas, is bound to repeat itself in Burma, thus creating for this country, too, a new problem of underdevelopment—unemployment.

According to OECD, unemployment, education, nutrition and income distribution (with the emphasis on unemployment) are the key problems of underdevelopment that foreign-aid programs have not begun to tackle. It would appear, moreover, that, if left to the United States Congress, they are not going to be tackled in the foreseeable future.

V. POSTSCRIPT TO COLONIALISM

EDITOR'S INTRODUCTION

The aftermath of colonialism has been a period of change and readjustment, of violence and peaceful accommodation. Belgium was convinced that its former colony, the Congo, could never function alone. It was mistaken. Britain, in relinquishing its colonies, hoped its political traditions would survive. Many did not. But, according to Sierra Leone's Davidson Nicol, a precious part of Britain's legacy does thrive.

Many ties, both economic and cultural, still link the new nations with their former masters. Of the whites who fled Africa or were expelled, many have returned. Moreover, they still enjoy a privileged position, according to New York *Times* correspondent William Borders. The "French connection," as *The Economist*'s survey of the Maghreb points out, remains strong—so strong, in fact, that an editorial in *America* refers to French "neocolonialism." Neocolonialism is also the theme of Obi Okudo, a Tanzanian journalist. In "The Second Scramble for Africa," he claims that the whites are bent on reversing the trend of independence through economic slavery.

Anti-imperialism is widespread, and not only in Socialist or radical countries. Together with neutralism or nonalignment, it is the basic foreign-policy tenet of a majority of the Afro-Asian nations, for reasons which Ernest W. Lefever explains.

Afro-Asian neutralism has proved to be a formidable buffer not only against alliance with the West but also against alliance with the East—with the Soviet Union and China. The Soviet failure in trying to fill the vacuum left by the colonial powers in the Middle East is examined by Walter

Laqueur, director of the Institute of Contemporary History in London and a professor at Tel Aviv University. Hammond Rolph of the University of Southern California explains why "people's wars" have ignited few fires in the developing world.

In the final selection, Professor Fred R. von der Mehden summarizes the main lessons of the postcolonial era and their implications for the future.

A BRITISH EMPIRE OF THE MIND [1]

Empires do not necessarily mean the domination of black men by white, nor do they always imply arrogance and cruelty. Over the past century the British Empire was one of many: the Dutch, the German, the Belgian, the Portuguese and the French. The last rivaled the British in size in Africa and Southeast Asia. The Ottoman Empire at its peak embraced territories in three continents. The Fulani Empire, a black one started by Othman dan Fodio, stretched from Senegal to the Cameroons and lasted for about a century before it was broken by the British and French. The empire of the Sultan of Zanzibar stretched over much of present-day East Africa.

I write this, as a black man, not to minimize the achievements of the British or to write an apologia (they do not need me to do that), but simply to point out that the holding of empires is a way of life, and that the great credit did not lie in their acquisition of colonies, which was often a military exercise, nor in their maintenance, which involved military occupation, but in their peaceful departure from these territories after doing an astonishing amount of good. During this transitional period there was a formal granting of independence after a brief and sometimes symbolic struggle and the imprisonment of leaders. In some cases such as India the

[1] From article, "Nostalgia for Empire," by Davidson Nicol, former High Commissioner of Sierra Leone in London and Executive Director, United Nations Institute for Training and Research. *Listener* (London). 87:237-40. F. 24, '72. Copyright © 1972 by Davidson Nicol. Reprinted by permission.

struggle was not so brief; in others like Kenya it was not at all symbolic but quite brutal.

Many Africans will deny that Britain granted independence willingly. They maintain that Britain was too weak after the 1939-1945 war to hold India and the colonies, and that when the British were forced to let them go they quickly and with a show of generosity granted political independence and substituted for it economic imperialism. This is in line with the school of thought which claims that slavery was not abolished by the European powers because of any goodness of heart, but because abolitionists like Clarkson, Wilberforce and Granville Sharp realized that it was more economic to abolish slavery and gain some political stability on the Atlantic coast of Africa, and so be able to exploit more thoroughly the vast African territories for profitable products like palm oil.

These newer and nationalistic interpretations involve two factors. The first is that no one likes to be grateful all the time. It is never in Britain considered fair, reasonable or in good taste for Americans to repeat that their intervention won the last two world wars for Britain and France, nor would it be entirely correct. By the same token, colored people cannot expect to be happy when it is pointed out persistently or subtly that they were slaves, and that, but for the kindness of the British Parliament and the abolitionists, they would not have gained their freedom; nor can Afro-Asians be expected to accept without some resentment an independence which they believe was granted them as alms are given to a beggar. There is a certain insensitivity in all of us which makes us feel that others should love us for doing good to them. But, as Oscar Wilde pointed out, a man finds it difficult to forgive someone who does him an act of kindness.

In his inaugural address to the United Nations . . . [in 1970], the prime minister of Fiji explained why, although entitled to design a flag in any way they wished, his newly independent nation had decided to keep a replica of the Union Jack as part of their flag. Although, he said, there had been imperfections and arrogance, and occasional injustice, there was something fundamentally decent about the British administration which made them want to keep a visible memory of it on their flag.

It is usually expected that nonwhite races will find nothing good to say about the British Empire. This is not so. Many Afro-Asian leaders now in power received their training and education after the Second World War, when the process of decolonization towards self-government had already started. They spent more time taking over and learning to rule than in recriminations about the past. . . . The governors who were sent out towards the end had clear instructions to bring the territories to self-government as quickly as possible, and their most difficult task was to decide on the inheritors. It was as hard to do this when the territory was racially homogeneous—as in the West African territories—as it was where there were different races. In the racially homogeneous territories, there was the danger of tribalism; in the others, racism. . . .

Many young Afro-Asians coming out of universities have only a vague idea what the British Empire was, and the same may be said of the young in Britain. Those of us now in our forties and fifties, who grew up in the heyday of Empire, marched in school uniforms on Empire Day, saluting as we passed the platform where the bemedaled governor stood surrounded by senior white officials and their wives. The odd black face who had made it sat with them as a symbol of the noncommissioned ranks of blacks and browns who had loyally served the British government and continued to do so. Even then, however, it was possible at school to differentiate the different phases of the Empire. The eastern flank of the United States had once been part of it, but was lost—and this seemed to have produced a willingness to give self-government to the white states and provinces in Australia, Canada, New Zealand and South Africa. India had been conquered militarily, and so were many countries in Africa and the Caribbean. Sometimes the territories had been wrested from other European powers, sometimes from the local rulers themselves, but, one way or another, the administration was backed by military force: a show of independence or a fight for self-government was quickly put down by armed force or by a show of armed force.

Yet it was not always so. In the nineteenth century many of the coastal areas of West Africa and of the Caribbean had black people in them, who regarded themselves as loyal subjects of Queen Victoria, and prayed that the benefits of the British Empire might be extended to the interior, to open it up for trade and quell the warring tribes. There was friendship between races, and wealthy Africans and Asians sent their children off to schools and universities in England, and entertained white colonial governors and civil servants to dinner at their well-furnished homes abroad. When Mac-Carthy Island, a trade center in Gambia, was exposed to attack from neighboring African countries, the local Africans and possibly one or two Europeans—hastily gathered and led by Africanus Horton, a black—formed a special constabulary which had to take an oath swearing that they would "well and faithfully serve our Sovereign Lady the Queen." Although a passionate nationalist with schemes to change the West African settlements into monarchies and republics, Horton, who was a Sierra Leonean of Nigerian origin, and a prolific writer, was fervently loyal to the Queen and to things British. He had been educated at Fourah Bay College in Sierra Leone and had graduated as a medical doctor from King's College, London and Edinburgh University in the late 1850s. The administrative civil service, which later became exclusively white, was at that time interracial and contained local men and a few of mixed blood. The local black and brown elite looked forward to an independence of the type which the colonies in Australia were enjoying as part of the great British Empire. A few of the very wealthy ones had Europeans in their employ. All this was shattered at the turn of the century when color prejudice supervened and reigned supreme for the next fifty years.

The period between 1900 and 1950 was the worst for race relations in the history of the British Empire. . . . During this twilight of Empire—to the British, it was the high noon— emotional tensions built up to exploding point. The few of the governing race who were hypersensitive could not bear these tensions and left for home to write about them—George Orwell, a police officer in Burma; [Edward] Morgan Forster, a tutor in India; Joyce Cary, an administrative officer in Northern Nigeria. Others passed through, observed them, and entrapped them in travel journals and fiction, like Somerset Maugham in Malaya and, at a deeper level, Graham Greene in Sierra Leone and Liberia.

The rising local bourgeoisie was becoming better educated and challenging the British for the few available senior jobs. Two wars, the Boer War and the Great War, had been fought and won, and had brought about great changes. Most British officials felt that there should then be a period of consolidation and of slow but steady progress under "native" rulers who were regarded as the rightful heirs of the Empire. It was at this point that British-trained natives started their serious challenge to join the administrative service. After some resistance, a few were taken in. But many of the British did not believe this was the right course: they themselves had taken over from chiefs and maharajahs and they felt they should hand over to them instead of to an educated but rootless bourgeoisie.

In a more maddening fashion, native lawyers trained at the Inns of Court in London . . . started harassing the local British officials. There was a whole galaxy or gallery of them, depending on whose side you were. Gandhi and Nehru in India, Mensah Sarbah and Caseley Hayford in Ghana, and their distinguished West Indian counterparts about whom not enough has been written. They challenged the British on legal grounds which only the few British lawyers in the territories, together with the legal advisers to the India and Colonial Offices, properly understood; certainly the local white officials never quite understood them. The people in question were clapped in jail, and branded as a bunch of subversives. But they won in the end because the British usually obey their own rules and the legal grounds on which they had based their challenge were indisputable.

So much has been recently written about the effect on Afro-Asian nationalism of the London School of Economics or of Sandhurst and Mons Officer Training School that there's a tendency to forget that its greatest formative influence was probably the Inns of Court in London, tucked away between Holborn and Fleet Street. For over a hundred years, brown, black and yellow men—and, increasingly, women—from all over the British Empire have proudly marched forward, black-gowned and bewigged on their graduation day, to be called to the Bar. They have then gone home to scattered lands, to introduce and uphold British concepts of justice. Some followed conventional pathways, made their fortunes and retired, weighted with distinction and decorations. Others fought the despotic authority of colonialism (and, later, sometimes that of their own people) in the cause of justice and freedom for the common man. A few came through victoriously, led their countries into independence, and were photographed at Buckingham Palace with the Queen; others died broken in prison cells, or in obscurity. . . .

It was not that there did not exist some form of law and order before the British came. But it was not formal and powerful, and it did not give scope to the young, the minorities and the poor. Whatever its imperfections in practice in the old days, British justice survived and was deeply implanted, whether by district officer or chief justice. It is now usually the hardest institution to destroy and the last to go when dictatorship supervenes in a newly independent country. And it is the first to return when despotism is overthrown. . . .

White citizens and white business are both safer under black majority governments than under white minority governments. Nationalization, expropriation and military coups in some African and Asian countries should not be used indefinitely as an excuse for prolonging or defending tyranny.

But, against these hard-core cases with which the British government must honorably continue to involve itself, there are the achievements of the granting of independence to vast territories like India, Pakistan and Bangladesh, with their 700 million; to Nigeria, the largest territory in Africa, with over 50 million; and to Kenya and Zambia in spite of powerful pro-white-settler lobbies and South African mining interests at Westminster.

There is a strong tendency in Britain and other European countries to continue to look back into the past. . . . This is understandable, and can be quite useful in reminding the young of the achievements of their courageous ancestors, such as Robert Clive and David Livingstone. However, it is in the future that greater glory lies.

There are many things for which Britain is outstanding abroad, about which those in this country show little awareness or pride. The power of the English language is one of the greatest assets that Britain has, and it can be used effectively by giving more financial support to institutions which foster it, like the British Council and the BBC Overseas Service. The British educational system is another asset. Whilst debates go on endlessly within the country about comprehensive schools and school milk, American, Asian and African parents write long letters to the heads of fee-paying schools and universities trying to get their children a decent education in Britain. Works of original research of great merit pour out in every field. Patients come from far and wide to seek treatment in British hospitals and are prepared to pay for it. Every single day, BBC radio and television produce features which in larger countries would be the feature of the week or of the month. The present and the future of the British Empire of the mind are more fruitful and acceptable to the rest of the world than the military or naval glories of the past which to others entailed pain and humiliation. . . .

Every thoughtful person understands how difficult it is for the British public and press to regard Britain as one amongst many, instead of as the leader. Even so, Britain is still expected to behave better and give more concessions than other Commonwealth nations. The British government sometimes shows resentment of this, insisting that they should have the same independence of action as Tanzania or Trinidad. This is impossible. Britain is a great power and one of the five permanent representatives at the United Nations Security Council. She is also a nuclear power, which none of the other Commonwealth countries is. She has the largest navy and air force, and still has some colonies. She must retain the responsibility in big-power politics to demonstrate Commonwealth ideals. Everyone had vaguely imagined that somewhere or the other these ideals had been described. But this was not so. The Commonwealth Prime Ministers Conference . . . [in 1971] in Singapore first put them down on paper. They should be considered by all who really want to know what the ultimate achievement of the British Empire has been.

In my opinion, in spite of its human imperfections, the former British Empire has brought the concept of universal justice for the weak and oppressed closer to reality for more millions of human beings of every color and creed than any secular institution the world has ever known.

WHITES IN BLACK AFRICA [2]

Late one night during the tense period that followed the civil war . . . [in Nigeria], a tough-looking soldier halted a British doctor at an army roadblock to check his identification papers. As the doctor fumbled for his wallet, the soldier rested the barrel of his rifle inside the car window.

The doctor, his sudden fear getting the better of his discretion, said sharply: "Don't point that gun at me!" The soldier, also reacting automatically, turned the gun down,

[2] From article, "For Whites in Black Africa, Uncertain Role," by William Borders, staff correspondent. New York *Times*. p 9. Mr. 23, '72. © 1972 by The New York Times Company. Reprinted by permission.

grinned shyly and, in quite a pleasant tone, replied, "Sorry, master."

The incident, which could have occurred almost anywhere in the four thousand miles between Dakar and Dar es Salaam, illustrates the curious ambiguity of the white man's role in independent black Africa.

A Period of Adjustment

In the decade since most of the continent became independent, whites have had to adjust to the fact that the power of state, like the rifle at the roadblock, is in black hands. All the new governments are proud, and some have been overtly antiwhite—even violently so. . . .

The thirty-six black-governed countries have perhaps a million non-African residents, most of them Europeans (the term is used here to include white Americans). They range from the business executives flooding into Lagos and Libreville to the teachers and missionaries in the swamps and deserts, but most of them are routinely called master (or *patron* in French, which means the same thing).

The term *master,* a particularly startling one to arriving Americans because of their egalitarian tradition, is used not only in address but simply as a synonym for white man, as in the message "A master came by to see you but you were not home."

The British, who taught the Africans to call them master in the first place, often maintain that its meaning has been modified, especially since independence. But in almost every country a white face still helps.

In Nairobi a black bank teller peers over the shoulders of four black customers to solicitously ask a white man, who is fifth in line, what he needs. At the Dakar airport, or down by the docks in Freetown, a white man is more easily able to breeze past the guards without the proper papers than a black would be. According to some black Americans, the difference is one of race, not nationality.

Death of Attitude Foreseen

"I'm damn sure that they search me more thoroughly at the roadblocks than they search the white guys who even have the same embassy license plates," said a black diplomat in a French-speaking capital.

Confronted with such impressions, an intensely nationalistic student in Sierre Leone stared into his beer for a moment and then replied that those who still say "master" and act as if they mean it are only remembering colonial days and that their attitude will die with them.

Nonetheless, children much younger than independence often move off the sidewalk to let a white man pass. It is common knowledge that a used car advertising as "European-owned" will bring the highest price.

Whatever popular attitudes may be, the black governments have put many legal obstacles in the European's path. It is extremely difficult for a white man to get title to real property in Kinshasa or Lagos, black Africa's biggest cities, and the Liberian Constitution restricts citizenship—a prerequisite to owning land—to "Negroes or persons of Negro descent."

Most of the independent governments are also trying to reduce their reliance on the foreign businessman. Asians are being roughly forced out of Zanzibar. A typical decree just published in Nigeria sets a deadline for black control of a whole range of businesses, including movie theaters and beauty shops.

Whites Still Flowing In

Yet some white communities—of "expatriates," as they call themselves—are increasing rapidly, drawn to Lagos by the oil boom or to Abidjan by its emergence as French-speaking West Africa's commercial center.

Even in what used to be the Congo the flow has been reversed and fifty thousand Belgians have come back; that is only half as many as there were fifteen years ago, but only a few thousand had stayed during the terror that followed independence.

"They shouldn't have left—there's a lot of talk against the white man, but it's largely rhetoric," said a European who was in Kinshasa, then named Leopoldville, throughout the chaos of the early 1960s. He became quite rich, reportedly by standing at the airport with a bag of dollars and buying property from fleeing Belgians.

The racial fear on which he capitalized grew out of the Stanleyville massacre, in which Americans were tortured and murdered, or the Mau Mau terror in Kenya. Now much of black Africa enjoys a fair degree of racial harmony. In West Africa it is possible for whites to live for years without feeling the hostility that has become commonplace in some African cities.

Black Africans are often perplexed by the white man— why, for example, he likes boating, which they assign to poor fishermen, or why he walks when he can afford a car—but they rarely hate him.

"It's because they always felt in control in West Africa, so they never had to hate," explained a sociologist who has studied the problem.

"The White Man's Grave"

West Africa, which the English colonials used to call "the white man's grave," has a climate that is brutally inhospitable to whites, who never came here in great numbers. . . .

East Africa, on the other hand, began attracting a flood of white settlers a hundred years ago, when the opening of the Suez Canal made travel convenient.

Whites are still prominent in such former British colonies as Kenya and Zambia, and no less a nationalist than Tanzania's president, Julius K. Nyerere, has white advisers near the highest level, which would be quite unusual in the English-speaking parts of West Africa.

The French-speaking states follow a third course: France is still actively supporting several of them and making the major decisions in most of the rest. White Frenchmen are everywhere in evidence, even in government offices.

"The French have paid the piper and make damn sure he keeps playing their tune," explained Richard West, a British journalist who has written a book on Africa's whites.

Social change has accompanied the political and economic transformation of the independent countries. In both the English-speaking and French-speaking parts of black Africa the number of white women married to blacks has been increasing. Such marriages far outnumber those of white men and black women, perhaps because white men are more likely to take their wives to their home countries or because African society is such that it is more difficult for women to meet foreigners.

In a country like Nigeria, where there is relatively little racial feeling, mixed couples can have friends from any group. But even here tribal traditions and family pressures sometimes force a man who has a white wife to take a black wife as well—and the second marriage can be the undoing of the first.

What is the white man's future in black Africa? The black man might reply: "It depends on you."

At an outdoor cafe in Accra . . . [recently] a middle-aged Englishman dressed in the old colonial style of white open-collar shirt, white shorts and white stockings sat impatiently rapping his pipe on the table to attract a waiter's attention as he grumbled about "the lazy blighters."

At a nearby table a Ghanaian journalist watched in amusement and then, picking up the thread of an earlier conversation, said: "I guess there's not room here any more for Europeans like that one. But the kind of white chaps who come to help us are still urgently needed in Africa. And as far as I'm concerned they will always be welcome."

THE MAGHREB: "THE FRENCH
CONNECTION" [3]

Although the legal status of the French in Tunisia and Morocco, which were protectorates, differed from their status in Algeria, which became part of France, French objectives in each country were the same. They were to encourage European settlers to colonize the land and to build French towns for administration and commerce. The crops that were needed in France formed the basis of agriculture: wine and cereals and later citrus fruits and vegetables. As French capitalism developed, the industrial companies and big financial houses moved in to develop and control the mining enterprises, light industries, electricity, railways and the bigger farms.

Officially in Morocco and Tunisia the French governed through traditional channels; but in fact their control was as direct and tight as it was in Algeria. They filled all the administrative and technical posts from senior civil servants to postmen. The Moslems retained their small holdings on the poorer land and provided the cheap labor for the French farmers and the French industries. They had no political rights. The settlers' economic system was based simply and squarely on their own self-interest. Profits from their enterprises which they did not repatriate were used to import French goods for themselves. Yet, despite this common pattern of French domination, each country has developed differently since independence. This is due in part to the differing length of the French occupation—they were in Algeria for 120 years, Tunisia for 80 and Morocco for 44—and in part to the different histories of each nationalist movement. . . .

France's relations with both Morocco and Tunisia have gone up and down like a yo-yo since 1956. The French held both governments responsible for giving sanctuary to Algerian partisans and for the fighting along the borders. And

[3] From article, "Maghreb; a Survey," by Michael Wall, foreign correspondent, in collaboration with Sue Dearden. *Economist* (London). 242:survey p 4-6. Mr. 11, '72. Reprinted by permission.

France, at one time, drastically cut down financial aid to Tunisia in an attempt to bring it to heel.

In 1962 Franco-Tunisian relations took another knock when, after trying in vain to get the French to evacuate the naval base at Bizerte, the Tunisians attacked it and lost 1,200 troops. The French cut down aid again in 1964 when the Tunisian government nationalized all land still in settlers' hands. Aid was not fully restored until 1971.

The Moroccans were gentler with the French, leaving the majority of the farmers and businesses alone. There were no Bizertes. But when the French granted Mauritania independence in 1962 the Moroccans were furious. The low point in their relationship came in 1965, when a Moroccan opposition leader, Mehdi Ben Barka, was abducted in Paris. He has never been seen again. Moroccan security agents, working with the French police, were held to be responsible. The French government demanded that King Hassan should hand over his security chief, General Oufkir, for trial. The king refused and France reduced economic aid until 1970. But in both Morocco and Tunisia when France tightened its purse strings the Americans loosened theirs. The United States was not prepared to give Moscow the opportunity of getting in first.

Eight years of war in Algeria, a million people dead, wanton, indiscriminate destruction and the frenzied flight of over a million French settlers should have been enough to rupture French-Algerian relations for good. But the Evian agreements promised massive economic aid and a French-Algerian partnership in developing the Sahara oilfields. A sharp reduction in the amount of Algerian wine taken by France and Algeria's construction of its own oil pipeline strained relations at the time. But it was not until the dispute over oil and gas royalties in 1971 and the subsequent nationalization of part of the French oil interests that relations between the two countries were seriously damaged.

For some reason, the French leave a more indelible mark than other colonizers. In the Maghreb it has gone right down to the roots. In each country the French set out to educate a Moslem elite. A few Moslems were taken into French schools, attended French universities and trained in French methods of administration. The young radicals were more influenced by the left wing in Paris than in Cairo, Baghdad or Damascus. When independence came, many educated Moslems spoke French better than Arabic; even today French prevails as a diplomatic and commercial language. The link between language and trade is strong: a Moroccan businessman will ignore a letter in English. If he has a choice he will opt for a French product because he understands French business methods and can get on the telephone and rattle off in French. And because of the language it is easier to employ French-speaking technicians, advisers and teachers.

Education still follows a basic French pattern and France left a valuable legacy in the modern cities it built, the network of roads, the ports, electricity and telephone services and the provision of medical services.

But the Maghreb countries were also left with massive problems. They were confronted with rapidly rising populations (a result of the progress made in preventive medicine) and enormous numbers of urban unemployed people—the peasants who had flocked to the cities when the settlers took their lands. They faced a terrifying shortage of educated people in the administration and in the professions, a lack of skilled workers and an aching need for financial and technical aid to develop natural resources. Moreover, they received their independence when the Communists in the West vied with each other to draw the developing countries into their own spheres of influence and at a time when the Arab world was becoming increasingly obsessed about Israel. These problems and tensions remain, but each country has sought to resolve them in its own way.

FRENCH "NEOCOLONIALISM" [4]

Lay it perhaps to the genius of the late Charles de Gaulle. Whatever the explanation, the one Western nation that has been leading a charmed life in the Third World is France. In many respects there happens to be very little difference between France's present relationship with its one-time African empire and Portugal's colonial relationship with Angola and Mozambique. And yet President Georges Pompidou can embark on an African tour that is taking him to five countries and expect to be welcomed as a father figure. As one British diplomat in Africa, mindful no doubt of the recent uproar over British arms sales to South Africa, recently remarked: "The French can get away with it, and we can't probably because they are still running their former colonies, and we sure as hell are not running ours."

Indeed, French armed forces are not an unusual sight in what was once called French West Africa. They serve as a reminder of the occasion . . . [in 1965] when President de Gaulle stopped in its tracks a coup d'état in Gabon and restored to power a government favorable to Paris. Even today French troops are actively involved in a rebel vs. government confrontation in Chad.

From the point of view of Paris, there is a considerable investment to be protected in West Africa. Economic aid, in return for trade preferences, is estimated to reach about $200 million a year. In addition to budget grants and development projects, France has over ten thousand technical assistants in government and education in West Africa. Where in Lagos, capital of the former British colony of Nigeria, the plumber or carpenter would be black, in Senegal's Dakar he is French. Most of the states of the former French West Africa use a common currency backed by the French treasury. Because it is convertible in Paris, it is difficult to

    [4] Editorial entitled "France in Africa." *America.* 124:167-8. F. 20, '71. Reprinted with permission. All rights reserved. © 1971, America Press, Inc., 106 West 56th Street, New York, N.Y. 10019.

tell how much of the money France pours into Africa eventually finds its way back into French pockets.

This surviving French intimacy with Africa has unquestionably managed to guarantee an amount of political stability. . . . However, stability has hardly been the hallmark of political life in independent Africa. One cannot help but wonder how long it will be before realism overtakes the fantasy world of French neocolonialism in West Africa.

Certain stirrings are already evident. Last September [1970], for example, at the meeting of the Organization for African Unity, French-speaking Africans dared to suggest that France was guilty of the same "misguided" policy for which Britain was being roasted in Africa—selling arms to white-supremacist South Africa. This unusual temerity suggests that the older generation of African political leaders, for whom the late General de Gaulle had a mesmerizing quality, is gradually giving way to younger men who are no more immune to iconoclasm than their counterparts elsewhere in the Third World. As the familiar problems of development—too rapid urbanization, underemployment, student riots—begin to hit French-speaking Africa (Senegal and the Ivory Coast, the two most advanced countries, have already experienced them), it may not be too clear that France is still "running the former colonies."

THE SECOND SCRAMBLE FOR AFRICA [5]

It is time "the sleeping giant"—Africa—woke up and realized that the second scramble for her is turning a full cycle with the approach of the centenary of the first scramble which was consummated with and consolidated at the Berlin Conference of 1885.

Since then much has happened, and after about a century of exploitation and enslavement, the famous "wind of

[5] Article by Obi Okudo, former editor of *The Nationalist* (Dar es Salaam), correspondent of *The Daily News* (Dar es Salaam). Reprinted from *The Nationalist* in *Atlas*. 20:20-1. Mr. '71. Reprinted by permission of the author.

change" has blown most of Africa into *de jure,* if hollow, political independence in the midst of economic slavery.

But recent events have shown that the white races are regretting their action in granting this independence and will stop at nothing to reverse the trend. This ought to compel developing nations to think positively, and that quickly.

The motive behind the present scramble is just the same as in the first one: the expansion of the influence of the respective white nations and the enhancement of the welfare of their peoples by exploiting the ignorance and economic resources of the peoples of Africa and other developing nations.

Self-preservation being the first law in heaven, as they say, it is only natural that the "big powers," while trying to expand their spheres of influence, would do all in their power to protect what they already have.

Whereas in the last century the method of acquiring spheres of influence ranged from "evangelization of and trade with" the indigenous peoples to bribing chiefs and at times exacting cession of their territories by coercion or getting their thumb prints on "agreements" prepared in Europe, the present scramble calls for a subtler approach if only because African leaders of today are literate.

The method is to study the psychology of the African leaders and use this to maneuver them and their governments into utter dependence on the big powers. The leaders, in order to live "up to standard," must earn as much as President Nixon (some African presidents earn more than £1,000 a month [$2,400], tax-free, plus a handsome pension on retirement), irrespective of the actual financial position of their countries, the gross national product and the actual level of wages vis-à-vis the cost of living.

And, in order to impress the masses that the leaders and their governments are working hard to improve things, magnificent buildings, new roads, hospitals, industries and even schools are put up through loans from the master countries and at cutthroat interests. In most cases, the industries are either entirely or largely owned by foreign interests. Even the budgets of some governments cannot be balanced and workers' salaries can't be paid without foreign aid!

But if, at any time, the leaders incline toward awareness of the oddity of the situation, they ask for trouble. They are either blackmailed into silence by a threat to withdraw all aid or they are overthrown. The leaders must be prepared to tell their people that they are poor and will only become rich when they are prepared to work hard.

One European, in a recent article, said: "Europe developed without aid, why can't Africa?" I agree with him even though we may point out to him that they had indirect aid from Africa and Asia in the form of colonial exploitation.

The basic factor is hard work. It took hard work, hazardous voyages and other risks for the Europeans to travel from their part of the world to Africa and Asia in the fifteenth century to exploit us. I can hear someone reminding me that they were driven by hunger and sheer necessity. Yes, but is our present plight, in which we find ourselves the butt of the white man's boots even in our own homes, not enough to spur us to accept the challenge—work hard and develop through our own sweat?

The zeal with which the West "protects" developing countries against "Communist contamination" whereas they themselves have every contact with the Communists ought to make the "poor" nations wiser.

That the central objective of all the scramble is economic is again illustrated by the panic and confusion which seized the West, especially the United States, at the election of the Marxist Socialist Salvador Allende in Chile.

Similarly, the invasion of Guinea by Portugal should teach Africa and her friends of Asia and Latin America many lessons. The fate of Patrice Lumumba in the Congo is a classic example of the fomentation of internal political unrest during which the capitalists rush in with troops "to protect" their nationals in the host country. And the United States was on the verge of repeating it in Jordan recently during the armed clashes between the reactionary, Western-oriented Jordanian army and the Palestinian commandos.

These weak nations should understand that the United Nations is for the big powers and their satellites. Is it any wonder that the Security Council had first to send a team days after the NATO-backed invasion of Guinea to find out whether President Sekou Touré was lying? The delay was merely to give more time to the invaders. How many teams investigated the situation in Cyprus before the UN sent troops to stop a civil war between two Cypriot communities —the Greeks and the Turks?

Because the United States is involved, the UN can't do anything in Laos, Korea and Vietnam. Instead, the United States carved each of these small nations into two, using the section it controls as a base to fight for the control of the other.

Africans ought to know by now that blood is thicker than water and that this is why the white nations stubbornly support their kith and kin in Southern Africa, not only to hold what they have but to expand where possible since the investment climate will be more equable for the capitalists where their "brothers" are in control than where Africans are.

No amount of protest, delegations and empty resolutions at the UN will stop the West from giving arms to and trading with South Africa, Rhodesia and Portugal. It is in their mutual interest to do so whatever Africans may think or feel.

At this juncture, it won't be out of place to suggest that serious thought be given to the desirability of retaining the Organization of African Unity [OAU] in its present form in which some of its members are no more than representatives of some European countries or settler regimes in Africa on a pan-African organization! The organization should be given some teeth, if it must continue to exist.

Honestly, I believe a more useful purpose will be served by the dissolution of the OAU or the pulling out of progressive countries like Tanzania, Algeria, the Sudan, Libya, Congo (Brazzaville), Somalia, the UAR [United Arab Republic], Uganda, Zambia and Guinea. These countries could found an organization which would be truly African and progressive and would work towards the achievement of their common desires—freeing Africa from the foreign yoke. If we wait till all African states think alike, we may wait forever.

With this organization, too, it would be possible and easier to establish a military pact among members and eventually a military high command which can, at short notice, move in aid of a member state and can engage the colonial troops who insist on perpetuating colonialism in Africa. The latter phase would strengthen the liberation struggle.

Some critics will quickly point out that breaking up the OAU or pulling out of it and forming separate organizations would weaken Africa and introduce unnecessary polarization. Yes, it would have been ideal to have had a pan-African organization like the OAU because "unity is strength," but where the OAU has proved cumbersome and ineffectual, isn't a number of smaller but more effective organizations better than none?

In recapitulation, let it be emphasized that this is the time for Africans to think and act quickly in joint defense of our rights; and, more importantly, for like-minded African leaders to come together and form a nucleus of an economic and military union. A future political union might be contemplated.

But *today* is the best day. Let someone like the great Mwalimu of Tanzania take the initiative *today*.

NEUTRALISM AND GREAT-POWER POLITICS [6]

Tropical Africa provides an off-center but not inconsequential stage for the drama of world politics. The larger significance of political developments in that vast area has

[6] From *Spear and Scepter: Army, Police, and Politics in Tropical Africa*, by Ernest W. Lefever, senior fellow, Brookings Foreign Policy Studies Program. Brookings. '70. p 12-17. Copyright © 1970 by The Brookings Institution Washington, D.C. Reprinted by permission.

been exaggerated in the recent past by the competition be-
tween the West and the Communist states for allies in the
Third World, and the importance of the African actors is
often inflated because the United States and the Soviet
Union seek to woo their votes on key issues before the UN
Security Council and General Assembly.

The black African states are involved in world politics by
necessity and by choice. Liberia and Ethiopia excepted, they
were created under the rubric of decolonization, which in
the liberal Western view is a fulfillment of the right of self-
determination and in the Communist view is but the first
step toward "liberation from Western imperialism." Since
Washington and Moscow were the two most insistent advocates of rapid decolonization, the new states tumbled into
the international community as neutrals holding a birth
certificate and UN membership card in one hand and reach-
ing out for a United States credit card with the other. Officially and formally nonaligned, all these states lean one way
or the other in the East-West struggle and shift direction
from time to time in response to changing internal or external circumstances. Since 1960 a majority have been moderate
and inclined toward the West. A minority have been militant, welcoming a significant degree of political and economic influence from Communist states (usually without
precluding Western diplomatic recognition or material assistance) and sometimes indulging in strident anti-Western
rhetoric. Mali, Guinea, and Ghana have been militant in the
past, and more recently Congo (Brazzaville), Tanzania, and
the Sudan have assumed that posture. Conversely, moderate
governments have been willing to accept substantial Western
advice and assistance, though they may receive some Communist aid. Liberia, Ethiopia, Senegal, Ivory Coast, Kenya,
and the Congo (Kinshasa) [now Zaïre] have been fairly
steady moderates.

African neutralism, like Asian neutralism, is a pragmatic
response to the realities of world politics. A neutralist leader
seeks to remain aloof from external struggles that do not

bear upon his immediate interests; he does not want his state to become a political battleground for two alien adversaries. President Jomo Kenyatta of Kenya once said: "When two elephants fight, it is the grass that suffers; and when East and West are struggling in Africa, it is Africa that suffers." Kenyatta's observation is selectively valid. Peaceful competition between Washington and Moscow, for example, has doubtless increased economic aid to Africa.

The foreign policy of African states, like that of the great majority of poor countries, is strongly oriented toward getting from the developed world all the material assistance possible, consistent with their political integrity. Some of their leaders have become adept at persuading Washington and Moscow, sometimes simultaneously, that a voluntary and noncommercial transfer of economic or military resources is in the interest of the donor state; this valuable state-building asset might be called "temporary alliance potential." The new African states have developed ephemeral and more enduring caucuses and blocs to lobby with the big powers or to marshal votes at the United Nations; such groups were particularly active during the first years of the Congo crisis.

Policies of Moscow and Peking

In this arena of competition, new to both superpowers, Moscow has had a more turbulent experience than Washington. In the first years of independence, Communist propaganda exploited the African ambivalence toward the West, accusing the United States and the former colonial powers of "racism" and "neocolonialism." In Ghana and the Congo, where Moscow made its greatest efforts, it attempted to "radicalize" the political situation by the classic Communist tactics of subversion, through trade, loans, military aid, and bribery. According to [William Attwood] a former US ambassador to Guinea and Kenya, the activities of the "Soviet KGB and other Communist intelligence services ... are both far-flung and intensive. Between 60 and 70 percent of all Soviet-bloc diplomatic personnel in Asia and Africa are intelligence agents in disguise. And among Communist newsmen, the proportion is even higher."

Heavy-handed Soviet penetration resulted in the expulsion of the Russian diplomatic mission from the Congo in 1960 and again in 1963 and was one of the key factors that prompted the military and the police to overthrow President Kwame Nkrumah in Ghana in 1966. These severe political setbacks, together with the widening Sino-Soviet rift, forced the Kremlin to downgrade its expectations in tropical Africa and to reappraise its policy and tactics accordingly. Since 1965 Moscow has not overtly supported direct subversive activity against tropical African regimes, but has channeled its weapons and training assistance to guerrilla groups, primarily those seeking to overthrow "white regimes." Though they are more pragmatic and less doctrinaire than they were in 1960, the Russians still supplement their diplomatic and trade relations with quiet, long-range infiltration efforts. Substantial investments of rubles and prestige have been replaced by behavior approximating traditional diplomacy, though there is no hard evidence that Moscow's long-range goals have been significantly altered.

In sharp contrast, Peking has adopted the revolutionary tactics Moscow has abandoned. China (sometimes with the help of Cuba, Algeria, or the United Arab Republic) supported the 1963-1965 rebel movement in the Congo. It has been active, sometimes with the support of the regime, in Nkrumah's Ghana, Guinea, Mali, Congo (Brazzaville), Burundi, Kenya, Tanzania, and Zambia. Red China provides material support and some political direction to the more militant guerrilla groups. It regards the Soviet Union and the United States as its principal adversaries and as the chief obstacles to its version of "national liberation" north and south of the Zambezi. Peking has encountered serious difficulties with the governments of Kenya, Burundi, and post-Nkrumah Ghana. It is the only one of the big powers that appears to have increased its political and economic investment in tropical Africa in the 1965-1969 period. (The Zambia-Tanzania railroad in East Africa is the most dramatic example of Peking's interest. The Chinese are building a thousand-mile rail line from Lusaka to Dar es Salaam at an estimated cost of $688 million in accordance with an agreement with Tanzania and Zambia signed in 1967.)

Washington's Recent Interest

The US posture and commitment in tropical Africa, as was evident in the Congo in 1960, is in part a response to the behavior of the Communist states and their allies. The states of that still "female" region are often the residual legatees of larger decisions. "The cold war has been the sinews of African diplomacy: if the United States and Russia were 'on the same side,' Africa's leverage on them would sink toward the pathetic level of its economic and military power" (R. W. Howe. "China as the Trump in the African Pack." *New Republic.* Sept. 5, 1964).

In terms of American political, strategic, and economic interests, Africa ranks below Europe, Asia, and Latin America, and Central Africa below the states bordering on the Mediterranean and located south of the Zambezi, particularly the industrialized Republic of South Africa. US policy seeks to augment the forces of stability and peaceful change as a means of maintaining the balance of power in the larger world and as a prerequisite to constructive economic and political development in Africa. To discourage conflict within African states, Washington opposes military intervention by other governments, African and non-African. The United States opposed secessionist Katanga and Biafra, staying out of both conflicts. It did provide military equipment and logistical support for the UN force that ended Katanga's secession in January 1963. Biafran secession was crushed in January 1970 with substantial military aid from the Soviet Union.

American diplomatic and aid policies are designed to strengthen the new states and encourage the development of moderate governments capable of responding to the needs of their people and of sustaining mutually beneficial rela-

tions with one another and with the industrial states of the
East and West. To this end the United States has provided a
modest amount of economic, technical, and security assistance, the last named including both military and public
safety aid.

While the political and strategic interest of the United
States in a particular region cannot be quantified, both economic and security assistance are significant indicators of the
importance of the region as seen by Washington. The US
foreign assistance program, according to an official statement
in 1969, is the primary means of expressing US interest in
Africa. The following comparison of economic aid (1946-
1968), military aid deliveries (1950-1968), and the congres-
sional authorization for military aid for fiscal 1970 in millions of dollars illustrates the relatively low US interest in
Africa.*

| | Military aid | | Economic aid |
	1950-68	1970	1946-68
World	$33,260.7	$434.0	$94,726.0
Europe	14,201.7	2.1	27,011.2
East Asia	9,747.3	214.3	12,154.1
Near East and South Asia	5,645.5	149.6	20,866.1
Latin America	687.0	21.4	13,087.8
Africa (whole)	218.0	20.5	3,923.4
Africa (tropical)	152.8	14.1	2,044.0

* From Department of Defense, International Security Affairs. *Military Assistance Facts.* May 1969; Agency for International Development. *U·S. Overseas
Loans and Grants.* May 29, 1969.

Except for Western Europe, which received the largest por-
tion of military aid in the earlier period, the relative ranking
of the regions is the same for the eighteen-year period as for
fiscal 1970.

The volume of US economic and security assistance to
Africa has leveled off since the mid-sixties, reflecting the
more clearly seen realities in the larger world and especially
in Africa. Like Moscow, Washington has been chastened by
the intractability of the African political problem and the

severely limited political and economic capacity of its new states. Both superpowers now operate under a more sober assessment of tropical Africa's strategic value, the reduced interest and commitment of each reinforcing the other.

THE MIDDLE EAST: SOVIET DISENCHANTMENT [7]

The basic problem facing the Russians in the Middle East—but not, of course, only in the Middle East—is that while they have become heavily involved politically and in some instances also militarily, they are not in full control of the conduct of affairs. Only ten years ago, to quote a leading Soviet commentator, "the stormy breakup of the colonial system and the anticapitalist slogans of many leaders of the national liberation movement created the illusion that in a very short period the overwhelming majority of the former colonies would go over if not to the Socialist, then to the noncapitalist road of development." It was thought that the obvious inadequacy of free-market capitalism to solve the basic problems of the developing countries would inevitably compel the leaders of the new states to choose socialism instead. ("Socialism" in this context, needless to say, means the Soviet model—not democratic socialism, and not the Yugoslav or the Chinese or the Cuban model.) The process of disenchantment with this thesis, which began around 1964, is usually linked with the overthrow of such rulers as Sukarno, Ben Bella, Modibo Keita, Qassem, and Nkrumah, all of whom disappeared within a short time, almost without a struggle. Even in those countries in which radical regimes, run by the army and/or a state party, had emerged, no one showed the slightest willingness to cooperate with the local Communists.

This was a blow, but its full impact was realized only much later. At the time some daring spirits in Moscow de-

[7] From article, "Russians vs. Arabs: The Age of Disenchantment," by Walter Laqueur, director, Institute of Contemporary History, London, and professor at Tel Aviv University. *Commentary*. 53:60-3. Ap. '72. Reprinted from *Commentary*, by permission; Copyright © 1972 by the American Jewish Committee.

veloped an optimistic new theory: whatever their professed ideology, the new leaders of the developing countries were building the foundations of socialism. If the conditions for "proletarian" (i.e., Communist) leadership had not yet matured, there was nevertheless ample reason for close collaboration with the new elites. The Soviets insisted on only one precondition, "internal democracy for progressive elements," or as Western observers put it, "licensed infiltration." . . .

Of late an unmistakable note of skepticism has crept into the writings of these commentators. That they should react sharply to last year's [1971] disastrous events in the Sudan, where the Communists and their supporters were savagely suppressed, goes without saying. But there has been growing criticism as well of countries in which the Soviet Union suffered no such dramatic setbacks. One author writing about Algeria concludes sadly that the agrarian reform of 1966 is largely a paper fiction, and that the political activity of the peasantry is weak or nonexistent. Another complains that political life in Syria, Egypt, and Algeria has yet to be democratized and that all the slogans about "handing power over to workers and peasants" are empty of content. Yet a third notes the "slipshod ideology" of the "progressive" regimes, the weakness of their links with the masses, and the fact that the task of creating "vanguard parties of Socialist orientation" has turned out to be far more complicated and arduous than was earlier anticipated. . . .

One of the issues at stake is the role of nationalism in revolutionary movements, traditionally one of the weakest points of Marxist-Leninist theory. . . . According to Soviet doctrine, nationalism is a transitory phenomenon (a position which may well be true under the aspect of eternity, but which is demonstrably useless in analyzing current events). However, Marxist-Leninist theory also distinguishes between the bourgeois nationalism of the West, which is thoroughly bad and reactionary, and the nationalism of an oppressed people, which is a progressive force if properly harnessed and exploited for revolutionary ends. . . .

Among nationalisms, that of the Arabs in particular has long been regarded by Soviet observers as a harmless aberration, to be viewed with tolerance. But here, too, there are signs of a change in attitude. "Arab nationalism," writes [Soviet author George] Mirsky, "is a particularly strong ideology which bases itself on history, tradition. . . . It makes use of the Palestinian question which is singularly urgent and painful for the Arabs." Yet, Mirsky adds, this ideology, an admixture of political and religious strains, creates a negative attitude toward communism which it regards as basically internationalist and atheist in character. According to Mirsky, even the revolutionary democrats in the Arab world are prisoners of this way of thinking, and only a very few—the brightest, ideologically most advanced among them —have so far escaped its pernicious consequences. . . .

Another issue which has greatly bothered Soviet policy makers is that of military dictatorship. All the "progressive" countries in the Middle East are now ruled by army officers. In the beginning (i.e., during the early and middle fifties) the Soviets had a hard time adjusting to this new phenomenon; even Nasser was attacked at first as a Fascist adventurer, in accordance with the Leninist doctrine that the army and the police should serve as the tools of the state, which is itself an instrument of class rule. But as Nasser began lining up against the West and increasingly began using Socialist terminology in his speeches, Soviet ideologists were mollified. After all, they now argued, class differentiation had not proceeded very far in the Third World, and the army therefore had to comprise a relatively independent force. . . .

Up to Nasser's death Egypt was the model country in which everything had gone right from the Soviet point of view, inasmuch as the "national-democratic revolution" had been extended and a "serious shift had taken place in the political thinking of the UAR leadership." (At the same time, a way out was always available in case of unpleasant eventualities, such as when a Nasser was succeeded by a Sadat. "Sometimes the leaders of a military coup are motivated less by patriotism than by a purely career-inspired desire to seize power," wrote one of the Soviet experts.) In general Mirsky predicted that not even "revolutionary democrats with epaulets" could cope in the long run with the tasks facing them, for their mental makeup was simply not attuned to developing the qualities necessary for political work and organizational activity on the highest level. Hence the conclusion that "purely military regimes cannot last long in the contemporary world." The progressive officers were bound to realize that the army was no substitute for political institutions, that they would have to secure the active participation of the "most progressive elements of the working class"—i.e., the Communists—and that they would have to mobilize the masses by establishing an avant-garde political party. At that stage their regimes would, in fact, cease to be military in character. . . .

These arguments were widely accepted until a year or two ago, when major setbacks occurred in precisely those countries believed to have progressed furthest on the road to socialism. . . .

The meaning of all this can be summarized very briefly: whereas only a short time ago it was assumed that in a very few years power in the Arab world would pass into the hands of avant-garde (Communist) parties, and that these parties would accept Soviet leadership, it is now openly admitted that the process will take much longer. One can well imagine that in private Soviet commentators are even more pessimistic than this. What prevents them from growing altogether dejected, however, is their belief that the political influence and military power of the Soviet Union will grow in the years and decades to come, that there will be a decisive shift in the world balance of power, and that as a result the Soviet Union will eventually be in a position to exert direct pressure on events in the Middle East. . . .

For the time being at any rate, Soviet policy makers believe in the wisdom of speaking softly while carrying a a big stick. They now understand that the situation is vastly more complicated than they had previously supposed, and that Arab nationalism, which on the one hand has abetted Soviet penetration into the Middle East, on the other has inhibited the further growth of communism (a dialectical process if ever there was one). The Russians know that military dictatorships in the Middle East, however radical their rhetoric, cannot really be trusted—but they have to continue supporting them for the present, until the time comes when they can more forcefully assert their wishes.

"PEOPLE'S WAR" [8]

There are important factors in the Third World which give a degree of theoretical substance to Peking's orotund claims about the universality of its revolutionary doctrine. Certain basic conditions, particularly in Asia, create vulnerabilities that must be recognized. Primarily, the internal weaknesses of the new states—political, social and military—make them relatively attractive targets for revolutionary insurgents. (They would be excellent targets for conventional aggression as well, but any such Chinese action is doubtful, especially in view of the presence of US military power in Asia.) Within many of the new states population diversity, racial antagonism and acute social cleavages arising from the modernization process produce centrifugal tendencies which could be exploited by insurgent movements. . . .

Why, then, when it is obvious that these conditions prevail in so much of Asia, Africa and Latin America, are there so few successful revolutionary wars of the Maoist variety? Why has Mao's "prairie fire" metaphor not taken on reality? Where are the "storm centers of world revolution" that Lin Piao so dramatically visualized?

In order to gauge the success or failure of Peking's universalist mission, we must consider the elements in the Chinese Communist revolutionary process, for these are basic to

[8] From " 'People's War': Vision vs. Reality," by Hammond Rolph, research associate, School of Politics and International Relations, University of Southern California. *Orbis*. 14:573-84. Fall '70. Reprinted by permission.

the model that Mao places before the Third World. This is best done by pointing out the stages in the process, since sequential precision is here of great consequence. The Chinese Communists claim that the careful development of each stage in a true Marxist-Leninist manner ensured them success in China and can do the same for others. At every stage, they assert, they carefully analyzed the "objective situation" and then proceeded on the correct path, always rejecting adventurous and romantic policies that might have led to disaster and developing a general line of theory and action from which they never deviated. (In view of the tumultuous and devastating "campaigns" and "surges" that have characterized Mao's twenty-year rule in China—the Great Leap, the People's Communes, the Great Proletarian Cultural Revolution—it is tempting to dismiss such self-assured statements, but it would be unwise to do so, for the theoretical framework remains, and the history of actual Maoist practice before 1949 lends much support to the model.)

These stages in the revolutionary process are rather clearly discernible and can be briefly described. The first step is the fashioning of a reliable tool—a hardened, united, tested Communist party. After the party has been organizationally consolidated and has developed its political themes, a move to broaden its base of political support is made through the creation of a national united front, a key feature of successful Communist-led movements in the so-called national-democratic phase of revolution in the nonindustrialized countries. When conditions are ripe, the party converts itself and its allies from political to "armed struggle"—the stage of "people's war"—which means not the abandonment of politics but merely an advance to a level of struggle where the final decision will be reached by military means. Following the rules of guerrilla warfare, this armed struggle is carried out in the rural areas by a peasant army, and is rooted in the Maoist principle of moving gradually from a position of weakness to one of strength.

As secure rural bases are developed, and as sufficient territory is consolidated under revolutionary control, an embryo rebel administration unfolds, and there is a gradual transformation of the guerrilla army into something resembling a conventional military force, which will intensify operations in accordance with Mao's three-stage theory of the evolution of people's war. As more contested areas are "liberated," it becomes possible to envelop the enemy's urban strongholds and ultimately to take them. With victory comes the final phase, establishment of the "people's government." It marks the end of the "national-democratic" stage of the revolution and the beginning of the "people's democracy" which, under the exclusive leadership of the party, will lead the country to socialism and at last to communism.

There are certain conditions that must exist, however, if this paradigm is to be applicable anywhere outside China, much less universally. In many areas the Chinese pattern is either not appropriate or would have to be trimmed to allow for serious deviations and variations. The Chinese themselves have been the first to recognize that their revolutionary experience grew out of historical circumstances in their own country which were in many ways unique, and despite the showy bombast of the recent period, they probably still accept the reality of this limiting factor. The question is, what and where are the revolutionary conditions likely to initiate a people's war in which the Maoist model would be the general framework for development?

The qualifications for a people's war devised from the Chinese formula are as follows:

(1) The cause must be a powerful one and must spring from indigenous sources. In his article Lin Piao clearly recognizes these requirements and their necessary linkage. He acknowledges that each people must make its own revolution and that insurgency cannot be successfully exported. Unless revolution arises from native political and social conditions, it will fail.

Furthermore, the catalyst of revolutionary upsurge must be strong enough to split the population, with the majority either sympathetic to the insurgents or neutral. The cause may be real or largely artificial, acute or dormant. If it is both genuine and acute, the chances for success are so much the better. However, we have seen in South Vietnam the great skill of the Vietcong cadres in generating ostensible support for an issue of little genuine concern to the rural populace (reunification) and activating grievances that long lay dormant (rural social reform).

One of the most potent causes energizing the revolutions carried on by the Chinese Communists and Ho Chi Minh's Vietminh was a combination of nationalism, anticolonialism and opposition to Western imperialist domination. Today these burning issues have lost some of their impact in Asia, at least in Marxist revolutionary terms. Aside from the struggle in Vietnam, the Communists have been unable to capitalize on nationalist passions lingering from the colonial era. Actually, nationalism in Southeast Asia tends to work against Peking, as the political and social problems of the resident Chinese minorities amply demonstrate. In parts of Africa, nationalism as a revolutionary issue exists to some degree, but in that locale forces other than the Chinese brand of communism seem to be profiting from it.

Despite the facile rhetoric of nationalism and anticolonialism and the easy assumptions by many observers of their paramountcy in the Third World, these factors would appear not to occupy the pinnacles of the mind and heart they once did. Issues of economic development, material well being, a fairer distribution of wealth, and a better life in general are beginning to compete with the old ideas of nationalism in popular imagination as well as elite concern. If this is so, would such issues support a revolutionary cause? Perhaps, but how will the Chinese example provide a spark? Communist China has undeniably made material progress since 1949, but Mao has compromised the prestige of his regime's early years by such fiascoes and aberrations as the Great Leap and the Cultural Revolution to the point where the attractiveness of his model can be seriously questioned. Populations in the new states seem increasingly likely to judge either conservative or revolutionary regimes by the material benefits they produce. Evidence supports the view that those developing nations which have achieved considerable material progress without revolutionary violence are becoming more appealing than Maoist China as models to others, e.g., Malaysia, Thailand, South Korea and Taiwan.

It might be interjected that the Vietcong movement is a deviation from the Maoist model in several important respects, and that lack of a truly powerful cause is a factor weighing against its success. If nationalism were an overriding issue and if reunification of North and South were a consuming passion among the South Vietnamese, it is likely that Ho Chi Minh would have won his war well before the Americans intervened in it on a large scale. The publicly stated program of the NLF [National Liberation Front] and its new provisional government differs little from the objectives expressed in the constitution of the Republic of Vietnam, and widespread cynicism and indifference are the apparent popular response to both. In the absence of a compelling issue around which to unite the people, the Vietcong have resorted to terrorism on an ever-widening scale, achieving a considerable part of their rural popular support or acquiescence through isolation of the peasants from the government by intimidation. In the special circumstances that have prevailed in South Vietnam since 1954, it can be strongly argued that the Vietcong have capitalized on chaos more than on issues.

(2) A second condition for the full applicability of Maoist doctrine is solid organization and unity of purpose in the Communist party of the country, coupled with the emergence of a dynamic leader of this "vanguard" at precisely the right time. This is the way events developed in revolutionary China and Indochina in the 1930s and 1940s, but do we see this kind of powerful vanguard party and leadership in Asia

today, outside China and Vietnam? Hardly. For example, communism in Burma is hopelessly split after twenty years of independence *cum* civil strife, and its most effective wing, the BCP (White Flags), has been devastated by a fatuous Maoist attempt to export the Cultural Revolution to Burma. The Communist Party of Thailand has never sunk real roots within the country or in Thai society and consists largely of a collection of sycophantic expatriates in China who dutifully mouth pro-Mao slogans on call. Even its role in the small-scale Communist insurgencies in several areas of Thailand is unclear. In Laos, the Pathet Lao would amount to little without the stiffening of North Vietnamese political cadres and military forces, while the real threat to Cambodia is not internal, but rather the presence of North Vietnamese armed forces on its soil. The Communist party of Indonesia, which was progressing well along a semi-Maoist road until October 1965, now lies in ruins, amid the bitter mutual recriminations of Peking and Moscow over what went wrong.

Indian communism presents a picture of splintering par excellence. The two parties which have competed since 1964 have now in effect become three, as an extremist group from the pro-Peking CPI (M) has broken off from the parent body in response to Mao's promulgation of an "armed struggle" line for India. Attempts to carry out armed uprisings in states whose coalition governments are headed by the CPI (M) have been largely unsuccessful and have been denounced by the CPI (M) leaders as "infantile adventurism," although extremist influence in West Bengal villages is apparently on the increase. Peking continues to encourage Indian peasant uprisings, but concedes "temporary" setbacks, partially due to "the absence of a Party which is armed with the theory of Marxism-Leninism and its highest development in the present era, Mao Tse-tung Thought, which is closely linked with the masses, which does not fear self-criticism and which has mastered the Marxist-Leninist style of work."

(3) Another requirement for revolutionary success is a weak opponent, or at least one so beset by various other

problems that his capacity to meet an insurgent threat is seriously limited. Since the insurgents are themselves feeble in physical strength vis-à-vis the incumbent in the initial stages, a slack, incompetent or preoccupied government becomes an asset to them.

This condition does exist in much of the Third World. However, it is probably subsiding as an asset to the Communists as the governments of the new nations take hold and begin to make some progress toward solving their problems. Furthermore, in some vulnerable areas, such as South Vietnam, weak incumbents are backed by massive outside power. Governments of many political shades are becoming more alert to the possibilities of insurgency. One of the richest ironies of the recent abortive Maoist uprisings in the Indian states of Kerala and West Bengal was the swiftness with which the CPI (M) state ministries terminated these episodes.

(4) Physical features of the area must not be overlooked. It is much better for the insurgents if the country resembles the China Mao Tse-tung describes in some of his elementary geography lessons: very large, relatively landlocked, with difficult terrain, a primitive economy and communication system, and a large population, widely and rather evenly dispersed. These geographic and demographic criteria exist in a number of new states, but none has the nice balance of all of them that China has. Many countries in Southeast Asia, Africa and Latin America have relatively small populations with considerable urban concentration, and many are accessible by sea. Despite the widespread notion that Vietnam is ideal for guerrilla warfare, its physical features are actually far from matching the Maoist model.

(5) A final requisite is outside support and sanctuary for the insurgents. Unless the incumbent simply collapses suddenly (as Batista did in Cuba), these are essential, especially as the guerrilla war moves into the later, more conventional stages. Lin Piao has stated clearly that "people's war" is es-

sentially a "do it yourself" operation. While support from Communist states will be forthcoming, he says, the insurgents must rely mainly on their own strength. Nevertheless, it is obvious in Vietnam that while Hanoi furnishes the manpower, the Communists would be patently incapable of carrying on the present kind of war without vast amounts of material aid from China and the Soviet Union.

China's commitments to revolutionary movements are in no sense open ended. Peking may be prepared to provide support in training, weapons, supplies and money, but only within the limits of what the Chinese leaders consider feasible in light of their assessments of the "objective situation" and their interests. Contiguity, or at least proximity, of rebel areas to the source of outside support is often critical in determining logistical practicability—obviously so in the case of sanctuary. Therefore, while people's war has been effectively supported by China on its periphery in Southeast Asia, the prospects for rendering such aid on the broader stage of the Third World are much less favorable. Peking harbors an assortment of expatriates dedicated to the overthrow of their respective governments, but their functions seem to be more ornamental than operational. (Despite the warm embrace of deposed Prince Sihanouk, it remains to be seen how substantial support of him will be.) In view of the low level of Chinese risk-taking in the past, any dramatic escalation in the assistance Peking gives to insurgent movements is unlikely. Mao seems to want revolutionary victory "on the cheap." . . .

One major impediment to Maoist hopes for the spread of people's war is the Soviet Union. The USSR's posture, both on its borders with China and in its diplomacy on China's southern periphery, exerts an inhibiting influence on Chinese revolutionary designs abroad. Moscow's great buildup of tension and military force on China's northern borders certainly has a deterrent effect; what is not so dramatically evident is Soviet activity in South and Southeast Asia aimed at countering Peking's policies. Despite continuing lip-service to the idea of "national liberation wars," Moscow has actively supported insurgency only in Vietnam (and even there for partially anti-Chinese reasons). Soviet diplomacy designed to strengthen relations with the governments of India, Pakistan, Burma, Laos, Malaysia, Thailand and Singapore has been accompanied by repeated denunciations of "adventurist" Maoist revolutionary war policies. . . .

Peking's reaction to Soviet policy has been predictably bitter. It rejects Moscow's charges of adventurism and in turn has characterized Soviet actions as betrayal of the revolutionary forces in Asia for the purpose of "encircling" and isolating the Chinese People's Republic. Peking has charged that Moscow, "in collaboration with renegades and scabs in this region . . . vigorously propagates the 'parliamentary road' in order to sabotage the people's revolutionary movement. It even supplies weapons to certain reactionary groups, helping them massacre the people's revolutionary armed fighters who are valiantly engaged in fierce battles. . . ."

RETROSPECT AND PROSPECT [9]

An attempt will now be made to point up a few of the more important trends. . . . The developing world provides a great variety of political experiences. The trends analyzed below are by no means universal but only reflect what appear to be the dominant tendencies.

1. While in most cases the institutions established out of the colonial period remain, the trend has been toward the development of political processes that have left these institutions with a primarily symbolic content.

In Afro-Asia, there remain parliaments, courts, elections, and considerable paraphernalia attendant to democratic institutions gleaned from the former metropolitan powers of Western Europe. However, with the establishment of one-

[9] From *Politics of the Developing Nations*, by Fred R. von der Mehden, professor of political science, Rice University. 2d ed. Prentice-Hall. '69. p 132-4. Copyright © 1969. Reprinted by permission of Prentice-Hall, Inc. Englewood Cliffs, New Jersey.

party systems, the increasing prominence of the military in civil affairs, and the decreasing role of political competition, Western institutions have tended to lose their original meaning. It should be noted that in all Afro-Asia only Ceylon and the Philippines have seen the national government thrown out and the opposition come into power by the democratic electoral process without a postwar coup. [Martial law was established in the Philippines by President Marcos in September 1972.—Ed.] An equal rarity has been peaceful change of government at the state level, with India and Malaysia being the prime examples.

2.   The trend appears to be away from organized, legal political competition and perhaps even from party politics.

Over half of the fifty-six new states of the postwar era ... [as of 1968] have political systems with no effective party activity or maintain a one-party pattern. We have also seen a growing number of polities making the transition from one-party systems to military control (for example, Algeria, Dahomey, Ghana, and Mali). Of the present military-dominated states of the developing world as a whole, fourteen had working party systems in 1960 while only four countries have gone in the other direction (the most prominent being Pakistan and South Korea, the latter going from civilian government to military and back to civilian within that period, while Pakistan's future is questionable).

Even Western democratic states such as India, Malaysia, Israel, and Singapore [and more recently South Korea and the Philippines—Ed.] have found it necessary to put greater political restrictions on opponents as a result of perceived internal and external dangers to the nation.

3.   The military is becoming an increasingly important part of the decision-making apparatus of the new states. . . .

The odds are now approximately fifty-fifty that a new state will have a successful military coup within the first decade of its independence. However, the prevalence of military coup is only one example of growing influence. Internal and external crises have increased the relevance of the military in civilian-dominated states such as Israel and Lebanon, while the large number of coups must lead those governments still under civilian control to maintain a wary eye on the military in their own countries.

The entrance of the military into the political arena does not appear to be necessarily tied to any one colonial history or party system. Since 1958, military coups have materialized in former colonies of Britain, France, the Netherlands, Spain, Portugal, and Belgium, as well as numerous states that remained outside the formal control of Western colonial powers. in Addition, coups have been directed against polities with no effective party systems (Thailand), one-party states (Ghana and Mali among others), one-party-dominant states (Bolivia), two-party states (Honduras) and multiparty systems (Argentina, Brazil, and Nigeria among others).

4. The trend appears to be toward longer periods in power for military regimes in the developing world.

While the "caretaker" pattern of military control has not been eliminated in the developing world, as has been exemplified . . . by Pakistan and South Korea, more lengthy periods of military rule are to be seen in all parts of the developing world. While a variety of uniquely national factors are responsible, partial responsibility must be given to the diminution of trust between military and civilian and the aforementioned decline in the support of democratic processes in the new states.

5. Economically, the developing world is not holding its own with the developed states.

A few simple statistics will suffice (and in the developing world few statistics are simple or accurate!) to support this statement. According to United Nations statistics:

(a) The developing world still depends upon primary products, and since 1960 there has been steady deterioration in its terms of trade as prices of industrial goods have gone upward and prices of primary products have shown a symmetrical tendency to decline.

(b) The share of world trade of the developing nations has dropped from one quarter in 1954 to less than one fifth in 1966.

(c) Whereas the United Nations Development Decade called for a yearly increase of at least 5 percent in the GNP of the developing countries, it has only been 2–3 percent owing to population growth and other factors.

(d) Public debt in the developing countries has risen from $10 billion in 1955 to $38 billion in 1965. Payment on public debt has risen from $1 billion to $3.5 billion in the same period.

(e) Foreign aid has dropped in the past fifteen years to significantly lower than the 1 percent of GNP that the developing states were called upon to provide at the 1964 Geneva Conference (it was 0.72 percent in 1965 and declining).

6. In the political arena, perhaps the central factor hindering economic development still remains the dearth of qualified personnel at all levels of administration.

Terms such as dictatorship, military domination, and mass party have tended to cloud over the fact that at the rural level the political situation is usually one of neglect, not domination. Not only has there been the continuing problem of insufficient qualified personnel (for which the colonial regimes can take a major part of the blame) but government tends not to reach the village level in a regular and meaningful fashion.

BIBLIOGRAPHY

An asterisk (*) preceding a reference indicates that the article or a part of it has been reprinted in this book.

BOOKS, PAMPHLETS, AND DOCUMENTS

Allen, Richard. Malaysia, prospect and retrospect: the impact and aftermath of colonial rule. Oxford University Press. '68.

Amin, Samir. The Maghreb in the modern world: Algeria, Tunisia, Morocco. Penguin. '70.

Andrews, W. G. and Ra'Anan, Uri. Politics of the coup d'état; five case studies. Van Nostrand-Reinhold. '69.

Bastin, John and Benda, H. J. History of modern Southeast Asia: colonialism, nationalism and decolonization. Prentice-Hall. '68.

*Bhatia, Krishan. The ordeal of nationhood: a social study of India since independence, 1947-1970. Atheneum. '71.

Brown, L. R. Seeds of change: the green revolution and development in the 1970's. Praeger. '70.

Brown, M. B. After imperialism. rev. ed. Humanities. '70.

*Cowan, L. G. Black Africa: the growing pains of independence. (Headline Series no 210) Foreign Policy Association. 345 E. 46th St. New York 10017. '72.

Crowder, Michael and Ikeme, Obaro, eds. West African chiefs: their changing status under colonial rule and independence. Africana Publishing Corp. '70.

De Lusignan, Guy. French-speaking Africa since independence. Praeger. '69.

Du Bois, V. D. Crisis in OCAM. (West Africa Series. v 14, no 2) American Universities Field Staff, Inc. 3 Lebanon St. Hanover, N.H. 03755. '72.

El-Ayouty, Yassin. The United Nations and decolonization: the role of Afro-Asia. Nijhoff. '71.

Embree, A. T. India's search for national identity. Knopf. '72.

*First, Ruth. Power in Africa. Penguin African Library. '72.
  Published in Great Britain in 1970 under title The barrel of a gun
  by Allen Lane.

Franda, M. F. India's 1972 state elections. (South Asia Series. v 16, no 1) American Universities Field Staff, Inc. 3 Lebanon St. Hanover, N.H. 03755. '72.

Gangal, S. C. India and the Commonwealth. Verry. '70.

Gardner, Brian. African dream. Putnam. '70.

Gifford, Prosser and Louis, W. R. eds. France and Britain in Africa; imperial rivalry and colonial rule. Yale University Press. '71.

Gulliver, P. H. ed. Tradition and transition in East Africa: studies of the tribal element in the modern era. University of California. '69.

Hanley, Gerald. Warriors and strangers. Harper. '72.

*Hanna, W. A. A primer of *korupsi*. (Southeast Asia Series. v 19, no 8) American Universities Field Staff, Inc. 3 Lebanon St. Hanover, N.H. 03755. '71.

Hatch, John. History of Britain in Africa: from the fifteenth century to the present. Praeger. '69.

Howell, T. A. and Rajasooria, J. P. eds. Ghana & Nkrumah. Facts on File. 119 W. 57th St. New York 10019. '72.

Kahn, E. J. Jr. The first decade: a report on independent black Africa. Norton. '72.

Kedourie, Elie, ed. Nationalism in Asia and Africa. World. '70.

Keesing's Research Report. Africa independent: a survey of political developments. Scribner's. '72.

Larkin, B. D. China and Africa, 1949-1970: the foreign policy of the People's Republic of China. University of California Press. '71.

Lee, K. Y. Commonwealth; a continuity of association after Empire. Cambridge University Press. '70.

*Lefever, E. W. Spear and scepter: army, police, and politics in tropical Africa. Brookings. '70.

Legvold, Robert. Soviet policy in West Africa. Harvard University Press. '71.

Liddle, R. W. Ethnicity, party, and national integration; an Indonesian case study. (Yale Southeast Asia Studies no 7) Yale University Press. '70.

Mansergh, Nicholas. Commonwealth experience; a critical history of the British Commonwealth. (History of Civilization Series) Praeger. '69.

Means, Gordon. Malaysian politics. New York University Press. '70.

Mortimer, Edward. France and the Africans 1944-1960. Walker. '69.

Owens, Edgar and Shaw, Robert. Development reconsidered: bridging the gap between government and people. Heath. '72.

Pearson, L. B. Commonwealth 1970. (Smuts Memorial Lectures Series) Cambridge University Press. '71.

Perkins, J. O. Sterling area, the Commonwealth and world economic growth. 2d ed. Cambridge University Press. '70.

Rapoport, Jacques and others. Small states and territories: status and problems. (UNITAR Studies) Arno. '71.

Ridker, R. G. Employment in South Asia: problems, prospects and prescriptions. (Occasional Paper No 1) Overseas Development Council. 1717 Massachusetts Av. N.W. Washington, D.C. 20036. '71.

Rosberg, C. G. Jr. and Nottingham, John. Myth of Mau Mau: nationalism in Kenya. World. '70.

Rotberg, R. I. and Mazrui, A. A. eds. Protest and power in black Africa. Oxford University Press. '70.

Scott, Roger, ed. The politics of new states; a general analysis with case studies from eastern Asia. Harper. '71.

*Shaw, R. d'A. Rethinking economic development. (Headline Series no 208) Foreign Policy Association. 345 E. 46th St. New York 10017. '71.

Turnham, David. The employment problem in less developed countries. (Development Centre Studies. Employment Series no 1) Organization for Economic Cooperation and Development. 2 rue André Pascal, F 75. Paris 16e. '71.

Von Albertini, Rudolf. Decolonization: the administration and future of the colonies, 1919-1960. Doubleday. '71.

*Von der Mehden. F. R. Politics of the developing nations. 2d ed. Prentice-Hall. '69.

Ward, Barbara and others, eds. The widening gap: development
in the 1970's; a report on the Columbia Conference on international economic development, Williamsburg, Va., and New
York, February 15-21, 1970. Columbia University Press. '71.

West, Richard. Congo. Holt. '72.

Woodward, C. A. Growth of a party system in Ceylon. Brown University Press. '69.

PERIODICALS

Africa Report. 15:18-20. N. '70. Burundi: political and ethnic pow-
derkeg.

Africa Report. 16:14-17. Ja. '71. Politics and power in Congo
Kinshasa. J. C. Willame.

Africa Report. 16:23-5. Ja. '71. Meaning of self-reliance for Africa.
Okwudiba Nnoli.

Africa Report. 16:14-23. F. '71. Nigeria's future. S. R. Pearson and
others.

Africa Report. 16:22-4. Mr. '71. What future for Franco-African
relations? Simon Kiba.

Africa Report. 16:16-18. Je. '71. Tunisia prepares for politics after
Bourguiba. Lorna Hahn.

Africa Report. 17:19-22. Ap. '72. Nonpoliticians take over [Ghana].
V. P. Bennett.

Africa Report. 17:14-17. Je. '72. Peace brings Sudan new hope and
massive problems. David Roden.

Africa Report. 17:18-20. Je. '72. Southern Sudan diary. Ahmed
Jamal.

African Affairs. 69:366-70. O. '70. Military in Africa. William Gut-
teridge.

African Affairs. 70:169-71. Ap. '71. Nigeria: the next decade. Sule
Kolo.

*America. 124:32. Ja. 16, '71. While aid falters, problems grow
and grow.

America. 124:139-40. F. 13, '71. Predictable Africa.

*America. 124:167-8. F. 20, '71. France in Africa [editorial].

America. 126:139-42. F. 12, '72. Meaning of Bangladesh. Jerome D'Souza.

American Historical Review. 77:463-72. Ap. '72. Partition of India: a quarter century after. R. E. Frykenberg.

American Political Science Review. 64:737-53. S. '70. Kenya's Africanization program: priorities of development and equity. Donald Rothchild.

American Political Science Review. 66:68-90. Mr. '72. Political clientelism and ethnicity in tropical Africa: competing solidarities in nation-building. René Lemarchand.

American Political Science Review. 66:91-113. Mr. '72. Patron-client politics and political change in southeast Asia. J. C. Scott.

*Asian Survey. 10:1070-80. D. '70. Race, leitmotiv of the Malayan election drama. N. L. Snider.

Asian Survey. 10:1081-9. D. '70. Communism, race and politics in Malaysia. Anthony Short.

Asian Survey. 11:121-30. F. '71. Malaysia/Singapore: problems and challenges of the seventies. Marvin Rogers.

Asian Survey. 11:149-58. F. '71. Union of Burma: age twenty-two. John Badgley.

Asian Survey. 11:677-92. Jl. '71. Multilingualism, politics and Filipinism. Nobleza Asuncion-Landé.

Asian Survey. 11:719-41. Ag. '71. India elects for change—and stability. W. H. Morris-Jones.

Asian Survey. 11:803-17. Ag. '71. Economics of the Burmese way to socialism. L. D. Stifel.

Asian Survey. 11:970-83. O. '71. New Malaysian government. J. R. Bass.

Asian Survey. 12:38-45. Ja. '72. South Korea: political competition and government adaptation. C. J. Lee.

Asian Survey. 12:56-68. Ja. '72. Indonesia 1971: Pantjasila democracy and the second parliamentary elections. Donald Hindley.

Asian Survey. 12:97-108. F. '72. Pakistan in 1971: the disintegration of a nation. Robert LaPorte, Jr.

Asian Survey. 12:177-81. F. '72. Burma: the army vows legitimacy.
John Badgley.

Asian Survey. 12:213-24. Mr. '72. Meaning of the 1971 Korean
elections: a pattern of political development. C. I. E. Kim.

Atlantic. 225:26+. Mr. '70. Kenya [report]. Stanley Meisler.

*Atlantic. 227:26+. Mr. '71. Congo [report]. Stanley Meisler.

Atlantic. 228:85-9. N. '71. Life of Accra, the flowers of Abidjan.
Nadine Gordimer.

Atlantic. 229:18-20+. F. '72. Birth of Bangla Desh. F. G. Hutch-
ins.

*Atlantic. 230:10-15. Ag. '72. Black Africa [report]. Stanley
Meisler.

*Atlas. 20:20-1. Mr. '71. Second scramble for Africa. Obi Okudo.

Atlas. 20:33-5. Ap. '71. Predicting Uganda's future. Winston
Berry.

Atlas. 20:30-1. Je. '71. Jordanization of Jordan. Yosef Akhiemer.

Bulletin of the Atomic Scientists. 28:4-5. Ap. '72. Bengal: balance of power revisited. Eugene Rabinowitch.

Ceres. 3:24-51. N.-D. '70. Unemployment—challenge to development; a symposium.

Christian Century. 87:1570. D. 30, '70. China; aid projects in
Africa. Hwa Yu.

Christian Century. 89:276-81. Mr. 8, '72. Cultural crisis in India.
L. S. Rouner.

Christianity Today. 14:40. Jl. 3, '70. Britain and race relations.
J. D. Douglas.

Christianity Today. 16:29, 38-9. Je. 23, '72. Burundi bloodshed;
with editorial comment. Donald Tinder.

*Commentary. 53:60-6. Ap. '72. Russians vs. Arabs: the age of
disenchantment. Walter Laqueur.

Commonweal. 92:157-8. My. 1, '70. Two, three, many Indias!
Kenneth Harney.
    Discussion: 92:326-7, 423, 490 Je. 26, Ag. 21, S. 25, '70.

Commonweal. 95:131-2. N. 5, '71. Passage through Botswana. Esther McCarthy.

Commonweal. 95:172-3. N. 19, '71. Detours on Africa's freedom road. Richard Gibson.

Commonweal. 96:189-90. Ap. 28, '72. City in Africa; urbanization and rural development. Jonathan Power.

Contemporary Review. 218:319-24. Je. '71. Morocco today. J. G. Farley.

Contemporary Review. 219:41-4. Jl. '71. Commonwealth co-operation. B. Narpati.

Current. 137:52-5. F. '72. Toward a new balance of power; India-Pakistan war and a new south Asia.

Current. 140:53-64. My. '72. Africa's new revolutionaries. Colin Legum.

Current History. 60:129-67+. Mr. '71. Africa, 1971; symposium.

Current History. 61:321-56+. D. '71. Southeast Asia, 1971; symposium.

Current History. 62:1-43+. Ja. '72. The Middle East, 1972; symposium.

Department of State Bulletin. 66:441-5. Mr. 20, '72. U.S. government and business: partners in African development; address, February 16, 1972. D. D. Newsom.

Economist. 238:i-xlii. Ja. 30, '71. Inseparable divorcees; a survey of Malaysia and Singapore.

Economist. 239:31-2. Ap. 17, '71. When Trotsky's heirs do battle with Guevara's [Ceylon].

Economist. 239:40+. My. 1, '71. Revolution fit for capitalists [Libya].

Economist. 239:43. My. 1, '71. Park—by a mile [Korea].

Economist. 239:43-4. My. 8, '71. War goes south [Ceylon].

Economist. 239:39-40. Je. 12, '71. Old Arafats never die [Jordan].

Economist. 239:37. Je. 26, '71. Heads must roll [Malta].

Economist. 239:45-6. Je. 26, '71. We're not a party, we're functional [Indonesia].

Economist. 240:18+. Jl. 10, '71. One cheer for Suharto's democracy [Indonesia].

Economist. 241:27-8+. D. 18, '71. India and Pakistan.

Economist. 242:38-9. F. 12, '72. Breaking with the past [Zambia].

Economist. 242:31+. F. 26, '72. India spans the old empire like a new colossus.

Economist. 242:42. F. 26, '72. Zaïre: dust to dust.

*Economist. 242:survey 1-25. Mr. 11, '72. Maghreb; a survey. Michael Wall and Sue Dearden.

Economist. 242:44+. Mr. 11, '72. Salute your rebel general [Sudan].

Economist. 242:46-7. Mr. 11, '72. Two steps forward, one step back [Pakistan].

Economist. 243:74-5. My. 6, '72. The common market's backyard [Africa].

Economist. 243:51. My. 20, '72. Les événements de Tananarive [Madagascar].

Economist. 243:33-4. Je. 24, '72. Sri Lanka: still no money, still no jobs.

Encounter. 36:48-51. Ap. '71. African balance. Horst Eliseit.

Encounter. 37:36-41. O. '71. Anguished thoughts on Bangla Desh. Dipak Mazumdar and Peter Wiles.

Encounter. 38:8-15. Je. '72. Aftermath of Empire [India]. John Grigg.

*Foreign Affairs. 48:712-25. Jl. '70. New Africa. Guy Hunter.

*Foreign Affairs. 49:111-21. O. '70. Tribal politics harass Kenya. Stanley Meisler.

Foreign Affairs. 49:187-200. Ja. '71. New tides in Southeast Asia. W. P. Bundy.

Foreign Affairs. 50:112-24. O. '71. Marginal men: the global unemployment crisis. J. P. Grant.

Foreign Affairs. 50:339-50. Ja. '72. Korea and the emerging Asian power balance. Pyong-choon Hahm.

Foreign Affairs. 50:698-710. Jl. '72. The subcontinent: ménage à trois. Phillips Talbot.

Harper's Magazine. 245:84-92+. Ag. '72. Bangladesh in morning. Laurence Leamer.

International Affairs. 48:242-9. Ap. '72. Bangladesh: why it happened. G. W. Choudhury.

International Social Science Journal. 23:421-34. '71. State formation and nation-building in East Asia. Joji Watanuki.

International Social Science Journal. 23:435-51. '71. Nation-building in the Maghreb. Abdelkader Zghal.

Journal of African History. 11:591-603. '70. Origins of nationalism in East and Central Africa: the Zambian case. Ian Henderson.

Journal of Conflict Resolution. 15:347-68. S. '71. Political instability in independent black Africa: more dimensions of conflict behavior with nations. D. G. Morrison and H. M. Stevenson.

Journal of International Affairs. 24:203-23. '70. Development and structural change: the African experience, 1950-1970. Samir Amin.

*Journal of Modern African Studies. 8:233-49. Jl. '70. Arabism, Africanism, and self-identification in the Sudan. M. 'A. al-Rahim.

Journal of Modern African Studies. 8:363-87. O. '70. Algerian revolution in search of the African revolution. R. A. Mortimer.

Journal of Modern African Studies. 8:405-24. O. '70. Political integration in Africa: the Mali federation. D. M. Kurtz.

Journal of Modern African Studies. 9:1-10. My. '71. Left and right in Africa. Immanuel Wallerstein.

Journal of Modern African Studies. 9:231-51. Ag. '71. Land reform and politics in Kenya. J. W. Harbeson.

Journal of Modern African Studies. 9:253-61. Ag. '71. The ideology of "tribalism." Archie Mafeje.

Journal of Modern African Studies. 9:409-28. O. '71. Prospects for Africa's exports. Ann Seidman.

*Journal of Modern African Studies. 10:247-66. Jl. '72. The roots of corruption—the Ghanaian enquiry. H. H. Werlin.

Journal of Politics. 33:1052-75. N. '71. Economic dependence and political development in new states of Africa. J. D. Esseks.

Journal of Southeast Asian Studies. 2:159-68. S. '71. Punitive colonialism: the Dutch and the Indonesian national integration. M. A. Nawawi.

*Listener (London). 87:237-40. F. 24, '72. Nostalgia for empire —Davidson Nicol writes about decolonisation and about a British Empire of the mind. Davidson Nicol.

Middle East Journal. 26:25-36. Winter '72. Moroccan political scene. John Damis.

*Nation. 214:134-8. Ja. 31, '72. Future of a subcontinent; Punjab, Bengal & the green revolution. Richard Critchfield.

Nation. 214:582-4. My. 8, '72. Bangladesh: fertile for mischief. David Loshak.

*Nation. 214:721-4. Je. 5, '72. Nkrumah: the real tragedy. St. Clair Drake.

Nation. 215:49-52. Jl. 24, '72. Price of development [Indonesia]. David Van Praagh.

Negro History Bulletin. 35:89-91. Ap. '72. Ghana: the forging of a nation. J. H. Harris.

New Statesman. 81:270. F. 26, '71. Letter from Kampala. Naomi Mitchison.

New Statesman. 81:804-5. Je. 11, '71. Letter from India. James Cameron.

New Statesman. 81:834. Je. 18, '71. Electing Indonesia's general. Francis Hope.

New Statesman. 82:197-8. Ag. 13, '71. Taming Zambia's whites. John Hatch.

New Statesman. 82:293-4. S. 3, '71. Battle for black Africa. John Hatch.

New Statesman. 82:880-1. D. 24, '71. Bangladesh's real battle. Rehman Sobhan.

New Statesman. 83:35-6. Ja. 14, '72. Reconstruction in Vietnam. Richard West.
    Same with title: Betrayal of the Montagnards. Atlas. 21:43-5. Ap. '72.

New Statesman. 83:68-9. Ja. 21, '72. Africa on the move. Richard Gott.

New Statesman. 83:695-6. My. 26, '72. Black African backlash. Suzanne Cronje.

*New York Times. p 1+. F. 28, '72. For Africa, a debate in many tongues. William Borders.

*New York Times. p 9. Mr. 23, '72. For whites in black Africa, uncertain role. William Borders.

New York Times. p 5. Ap. 25, '72. Dakar spreading idea of black culture. Marvine Howe.

New York Times. p 9. Ap. 30, '72. Focus is shifted by African group. Marvine Howe.

New York Times. p 10. Jl. 17, '72. French influence pervades Marxist Congo. Marvine Howe.

New York Times. p 3. Ag. 14, '72. India, 25 years old, is showing pride as a nation. Robert Trumbull.

New York Times. p 2. Ag. 26, '72. Abrupt shifts mark Amin rule of Uganda. Bernard Weinraub.

*New York Times. p 27+. S. 2, '72. Nigeria moves boldly to gain control of her economy. T. A. Johnson.

New York Times. p E 2. S. 10, '72. Chad: a small but real war. Andreas Freund.

New York Times. p 15. S. 14, '72. Nigerian urges uses of the past. T. A. Johnson.

New York Times. p 1+. S. 23, '72. Manila sets martial law after attack on minister; social troubles deepen. Tillman Durdin.

New York Times. p XX 1+. O. 8, '72. The people who lived it recall democratic India's imperial past. Anees Jung.

*New York Times. p 4. O. 12, '72. The situation in Idi Amin's Uganda: unpredictability is the order of the day. Charles Mohr.

New York Times Magazine. p 18-20+. Ap. 23, '72. Algerians intend to go it alone, raise hell, hold out and grow. E. R. F. Sheehan.

New York Times Magazine. p 16-17+. My. 14, '72. Nine years after a fateful assassination, the cult of Diem. Robert Shaplen.

New York Times Magazine. p 7+. Je. 25, '72. Bhutto picks up the pieces of Pakistan. J. P. Sterba.

New York Times Magazine. p 10-11+. Ag. 6, '72. Why Sadat packed off the Russians. E. R. F. Sheehan.

*New York Times Magazine. p 16-17+. O. 1, '72. The cult of Kim. Mark Gayn.

New Yorker. 47:42-8+. O. 16; 47-54+. O. 23; 53-8+. O. 30, '71. Profiles: Julius Kambarage Nyerere. W. E. Smith.

New Yorker. 47:40-2+. F. 12; 89-96+. F. 19, '72. Reporter at large [Bangladesh]. Robert Shaplen.

New Yorker. 48:58+. Ag. 12, '72. Letter from Hanoi. Joseph Kraft.

Newsweek. 75:39-40. My. 4, '70. Turmoil in the Caribbean.

Newsweek. 78:61-2. N. 22, '71. C'est si bon [Swaziland].

Newsweek. 79:32. Ja. 24, '72. End of an experiment [Ghana].

Newsweek. 79:34. Ja. 24, '72. Great purge [Guinea].

Newsweek. 79:35-9. Mr. 27, '72. Bangladesh: the fight for survival; with report by Arnaud de Borchgrave.

Newsweek. 79:42. Ap. 3, '72. Talk with Pakistan's President Bhutto; remarks. Z. A. Bhutto.

Newsweek. 79:33-4+. Ap. 10, '72. Perils of Pakistan.

*Newsweek. 79:39-40. Je. 26, '72. Slaughter of the Hutus [Burundi].

Newsweek. 80:36+. Ag. 14, '72. Thou shalt not steal! [Central African Republic]

*Newsweek. 80:36+. S. 11, '72. Libya: the desert upstart. Loren Jenkins.

Newsweek. 80:38. S. 11, '72. Sudan: the spoils of war.

*Orbis. 14:572-87. Fall '70. "People's war": vision vs. reality. Hammond Rolph.

Orbis. 14:714-39. Fall '70. Iraqi revolution: a case study of army rule. P. A. Marr.

*Orbis. 15:1109-21. Winter '72. New order in South Asia. N. D. Palmer.

Orbis. 16:174-210. Spring '72. Indonesia, the Netherlands and the "Republic of the South Moluccas." J. M. van der Kroef.

Pacific Affairs. 44:173-92. Summer '71. Post-independence nationalism in south and southeast Asia: a reconsideraiton. Rupert Emerson.

Pacific Affairs. 44:193-210. Summer '71. Politics of regionalism in India. L. P. Fickett, Jr.

Pacific Affairs. 44:337-52. Fall '71. Colonialism, social structure and nationalism: the Philippine case. Martin Meadows.

Pacific Affairs. 45:42-59. Spring '72. Indonesian nationalism reconsidered. J. M. van der Kroef.

Pacific Affairs. 45:60-74. Spring '72. Burmese socialism: economic problems of the first decade. L. D. Stifel.

Pacific Affairs. 45:206-19. Summer '72. Military politics under Indonesia's new order. Harold Crouch.

Political Quarterly. 42:294-305. Jl. '71. India: retrospect and prospect. N. C. B. R. Chaudhury.

Political Quarterly. 43:187-200. Ap. '72. Pakistani post-mortem and the roots of Bangladesh. W. H. Morris-Jones.

Political Studies. 19:284-93. S. '71. Political parties in non-Communist Asia. James Jupp.

Public Opinion Quarterly. 34:360-70. Fall '70. Social rank and nationalism: some African data. Immanuel Wallerstein and Michael Hechter.

Ramparts. 10:28-31. Ap. '72. Apartheid in the new Africa. Ruth First.

Reader's Digest. 100:142-6. Ja. '72. Storm warnings in the Caribbean; social and economic unrest. C. T. Rowan and D. M. Mazie.

Round Table. 60:385-617. N. '70. Empire to Commonwealth 1910-1970.

Round Table. 241:71-81. Ja. '71. Common market's African associates. Kaye Whiteman.

Round Table. 242:199-207. Ap. '71. France and Francophonie. Edward Mortimer.

Round Table. 244:431-594. O. '71. Britain, the Commonwealth and Europe.

Round Table. 244:507-10. O. '71. Commonwealth South Asia and the enlarged Community. Sisir Gupta.

Round Table. 244:515-21. O. '71. Commonwealth Africa and the enlarged Community. Roy Lewis.

Round Table. 246:241-8. Ap '72. Political transformation in Ceylon. A. J. Wilson.

Scientific American. 266:15-21. Ap. '72. Political factors in economic assistance. K. G. Myrdal.

Senior Scholastic. 100:4-8+. Mr. 6, '72. Bangla Desh: picking up the pieces.

Time. 97:37-8+. F. 1, '71. Black Africa a decade later.

Time. 99:27. Ja. 24, '72. Zaïrization of almost everything.

Time. 99:27. Ja. 31, '72. Week-old baby; government of I. Acheampong [Ghana].

Time. 99:30. My. 22, '72. Revolt of the Hutu [Burundi].

Time. 99:34. My. 29, '72. Triste just society [Algeria].

Time. 99:33. Je. 12, '72. Revenge of the Tutsis; revolt of Hutu tribal majority [Burundi].

Time. 100:22-3. Ag. 21, '72. Unwanted [Asians in Uganda].

Time. 100:23. Ag. 21, '72. Jamaican Joshua [Michael Manley].

U.S. News & World Report. 68:63-4. My. 25, '70. Good news from Asia: India is beginning to move.

*U.S. News & World Report. 69:52-5. Jl. 6, '70. Up from chaos: black Africa after 10 years of freedom. A. J. Meyers.

U.S. News & World Report. 71:12-13. D. 20, '71. Hindus vs. Moslems: conflict that goes back 450 years.

U.S. News & World Report. 71:43-4. D. 20, '71. Oil-rich Libya, is revolution turning sour?

U.S. News & World Report. 72:72-5. Ap. 3, '72. From revolution to reality: birth pangs of a nation, report from Bangladesh. J. N. Wallace.

U.S. News & World Report. 73:45-6. Ag. 14, '72. As Russians leave Egypt, who gains, who loses.

U.S. News & World Report. 73:16-18+. S. 18, '72. Arab terrorism, outraged world seeks an answer.

UNESCO Courier. 24:25-6+. Ja. '71. Independence of Africa and cultural decolonization. James Ngugi.

Vital Speeches of the Day. 38:261-4. F. 15, '72. Aid to Africa; address, January 22, 1972. D. D. Newsom.
    Same: Department of State Bulletin. 66:199-205. F. 14, '72.

*Wall Street Journal. p 8. Ag. 29, '72. Hastings Banda, offbeat nationalist. Ray Vicker.

Wall Street Journal. p 1+. S. 1, '72. Manila mystery: an abandoned boat is the key to a puzzle without any solution. P. R. Kann.

*Wall Street Journal. p 1+. O. 11, '72. The new Manila: Marcos' martial law is not very martial—but is it justified? P. R. Kann.

*Washington Post. p B 5. Ap. 9, '72. A time of testing for Nyerere's socialist vision. Jim Hoagland.

*Washington Post. p A 29-30. Ag. 9, '70. Peasant revolt cuts Senegal's vital peanut crop. Jim Hoagland.

World Today. 27:40-6. Ja. '71. Clan loyalties and Socialist doctrine in the People's Republic of the Congo. J. M. Lee.

World Today. 27:310-18. Jl. '71. Israel, the Arabs, and British responsibilities. Sir Anthony Buzzard.

World Today. 28:108-16. Mr. '72. Indian subcontinent after the war. W. Klatt.

World Today. 28:181-8. Ap. '72. Better outlook for Sudan. Peter Kilner.

World Today. 28:189-95. My. '72. Mintoff's Malta: problems of independence. J. Dowdall.